KEEP IN TOUCH

Contemporary Design for Invitations, Postcards, Stamps & Seals

GINGKO PRESS

Keep In Touch

Contemporary Design for Invitations, Postcards, Stamps & Seals

First Published in the USA and in Europe in 2020 by

GINGKO PRESS

Gingko Press, Inc.
2332 Fourth Street Suite E
Berkeley, CA 94710 USA
Tel: (510) 898 1195
Fax: (510) 898 1196
Email: books@gingkopress.com
www.gingkopress.com

Gingko Press Verlags GmbH
Schulterblatt 58
D-20357 Hamburg / Germany
Tel: +49 (0)40-291425
Fax: +49 (0)40-291055
Email: gingkopress@t-online.de

ISBN 978-3-943330-51-9

By arrangement with
Sandu Publishing Co., Ltd.

SANDU PUBLISHING ☰ 360

Copyright © 2020 by Sandu Publishing
First published in 2020 by Sandu Publishing

Sponsored by Design 360° — Concept & Design Magazine
Edited and produced by Sandu Publishing Co., Ltd.
Book design, concepts & art direction by Sandu Publishing Co., Ltd.

Chief Editor: Wang Shaoqiang
Executive Editor: Anton Tan
Copy Editor: Kim Curtis
Designer: Pan Yuhua
Sales Manager: Deng Baoyi

Cover Design: Pan Yuhua
Front cover projects by The Workbench, Quatrième Étage, Jay Cover
and Marka Collective
Back cover projects by kissmiklos, TSUBAKI STUDIO, Balmer Hählen
and Blürbstudio

info@sandupublishing.com
sales@sandupublishing.com
www.sandupublishing.com

Printed and bound in China

Contents

Postcards

Stamps

⛭ Seals

Preface

Dear strangers and fellow mail lovers,

I'm writing today to talk about mail—those small or sometimes big pieces of paper that often make you smile. There is nothing better than writing you a letter about mail. It has been more than five years since I wrote my last letter by hand. I used to send a lot of mail when I was young and the most interesting part was to use pages of my mother's magazines to make unique envelopes.

I'm a bit nostalgic at this moment, aren't you? After taking the time to choose a nice pen and a good piece of writing paper, you sat down on a Sunday afternoon, gathered your thoughts and wrote them down. And then you stuck a stamp on your hand-made envelope and went to mail it at the post office. We used to have time to think and do these things. But, nowadays, instant communication barely gives us time to react. Just one click or tap can open up a world that seems familiar, but, paradoxically, strange to you. You may receive information from people you don't even know. However, letters can give you a chance to slow down the pace and focus on a crafted object. It seems we have lost the ritual of mail in our daily lives.

Some may say that with the digitalization of communication, the world is going paperless. Don't fear, my friends. We are far from a paperless world! Paper has never been used as much as today. Indeed, paper is not often fully utilized because it is regarded as a disposable material. Fortunately, the paper-making industry was the first one to use recycling technology. And we are also witnessing the revival of paper. Today's producers are stretching paper's limits and creating new possibilities. Paper can be thermal, washable, tear-proof, metallic, translucent, velvety, glossy or even embroidered.

Paper is full of hidden characteristics. As designers and artists, we must rediscover them and reveal paper's incredible potential. That is what we do when we design mail art. We transform what may seem common and uninspired into something memorable, smart or even quirky. To break people's natural thinking about a piece of mail or paper, we need to create a sense of wonder in these everyday things.

My favorite part of mail design is spontaneous creativity and freedom that I cannot easily find anywhere else. Compared to corporate design, which can be stricter with brand guidelines and generalized usage, mail design sells fun. Even if it is part of an overall brand, a marketing communication concept or a special event, the elements of mail design can bring the brand to life in a social context and grab the recipients' attention with fun and excitement. Playing with different kinds of media, illustration styles, typography and printing techniques, designers and artists can explore the various possibilities of artful mail design.

Every piece of mail contains a miniature story and our job is to craft it through techniques and materials available to us. Each detail matters—the envelope, the stamp, the seal and the printing process of the paper. These details are crucial for us to create a mystery or a drama. Receiving a mail is not only a one-time action, but it requires visual participation. So, to appeal to the recipient, we need to build up the visual language.

The works we design are also sensitive because we work directly on something tangible. When they open the envelope and read the content, recipients become part of the process. Reading, touching and sometimes smelling it, the recipient will give weight and life to the letter. Meanwhile, smiling, laughing, crying or remembering after reading will give it a soul. Emotion is the key. It is what inspires us, but mostly what you should inspire.

Understanding a letter is not as same as reading an e-mail. Texting, tweeting and e-mailing is all about speed and efficiency. Most of the time, you even do multiple things while reading or sending them. Texts or e-mails are rarely lost because you can easily find them on your phones, computers or the cloud servers, when needed. A letter is ephemeral. If you lose it, you may lose it forever. And this makes a letter so precious. If it's saved as a collectible or souvenir instead of just being chucked into the garbage after it's read, you have already done a great job.

So dear unknown designers, students and fellow mail lovers, I wish you a wonderful trip through *Keep in Touch: Contemporary Design for Invitations, Postcards, Stamps & Seals*. Here, you will meet designers from all over the world, people who have challenged mail design and succeeded in making it a real specialization in the graphic design area. So open your eyes and let's design!

Designly yours,
Audrey from Allons-y Alonso,
a design studio in France.

INVITATIONS

Invitations are traditionally used in big life events: weddings, anniversaries and family birthdays. Written invitations date back to the Middle Ages when they were popular among wealthier families. With the development of printing technology, the postal system and graphic design, invitations became more widely used for different purposes like cultural events and commercial activities. What's more, creative designers can now blend 3D form and different materials into an invitation's design.

Gaming Technology
Show Invitation

✉

Design: Quentin Li

This invitation prominently features the graphic identity of an event with its specific visual language—the concrete angle, refined panel and accent highlight. The monochrome matte black sandblasting aluminum with sharp diamond-cut highlight gives a spirit of craftsmanship. On the other hand, the vivid cyan blue accent color on the cardboard gives it a sleek sci-fi appearance. All in all, the design conveys a seriously cool futuristic visual perception that echoes the brand image.

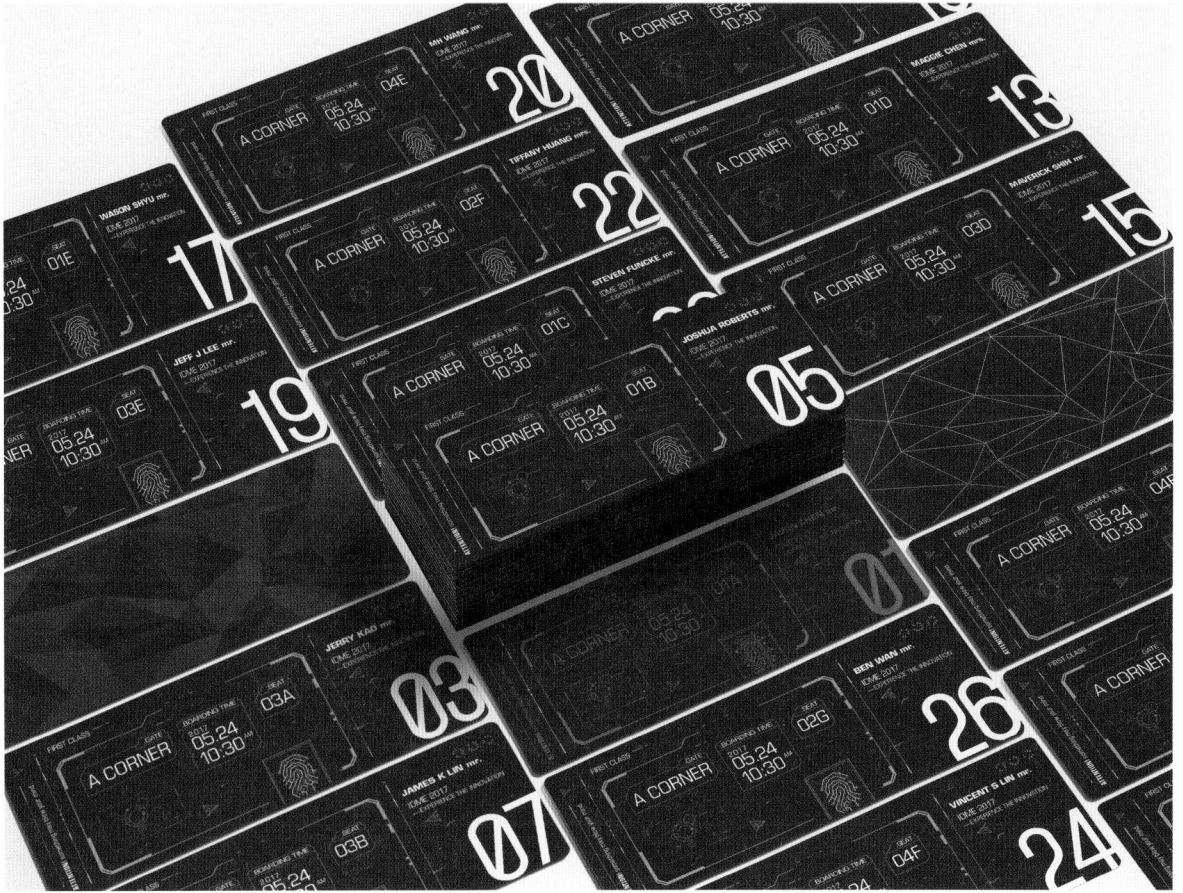

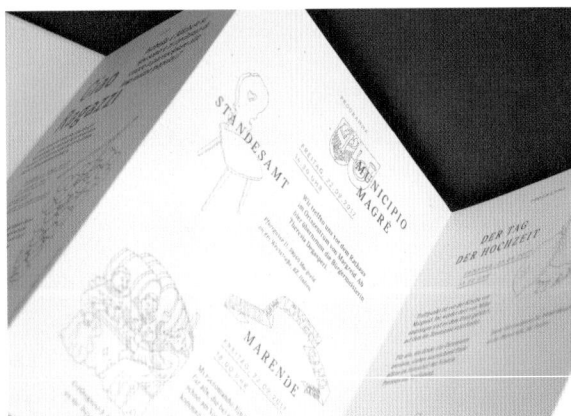

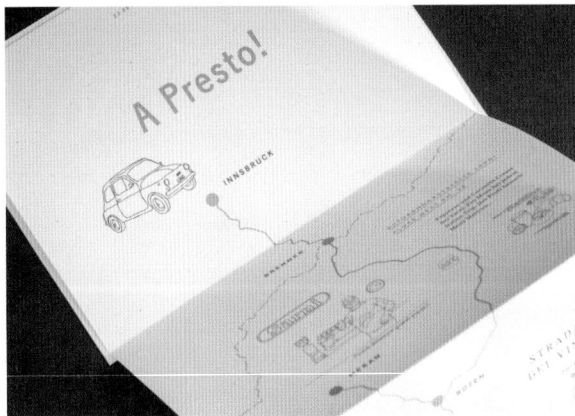

Tiamo—IXM
Wedding Invitation

✉

Design Agency: Bureau Rabensteiner
Illustration: Isabella Rabensteiner
Design: Mike Rabensteiner
Photography: Mike Rabensteiner

On the occasion of the wedding of Isabella and Mike Rabensteiner, they took their loved ones to the place where, more than anywhere else, they loved to be. The invitations illustrate the journey, the spots and, above all else, the feeling of love that wafts through the air. The whole wedding set includes high-quality invitations with hot foil embossing, envelopes, labels and a small website, along with the place cards, seating plans and thank-you notes.

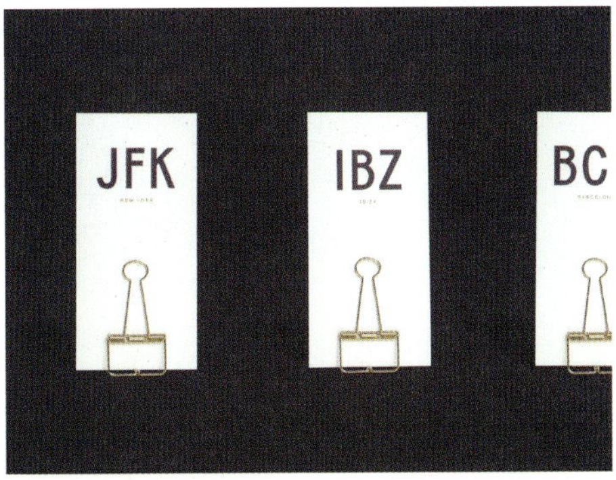

JFK IBZ BC

CAMPARI

SPONSORED BY CAMPARI

A Presto!

ISABELLA UND MIKE
MARGREID
AN DER WEINSTRASSE

To the Arnold Family
31 Lambton Road
Raynes Park, London
SW20 0LW, UK

SÜDTIROL
ALTO ADIGE

PARIS   LONDON
CDG   GAT   DUB   DUBLIN

BARCELONA
BCN   VCE   JFK   NEW YORK

STOCKHOLM
ARN   INN   AMS   AMSTERDAM

IBIZA   BERLIN
IBZ   TXL   MUC   MUNICH

VIE   VIENNA

SPONSORED BY CAMPARI

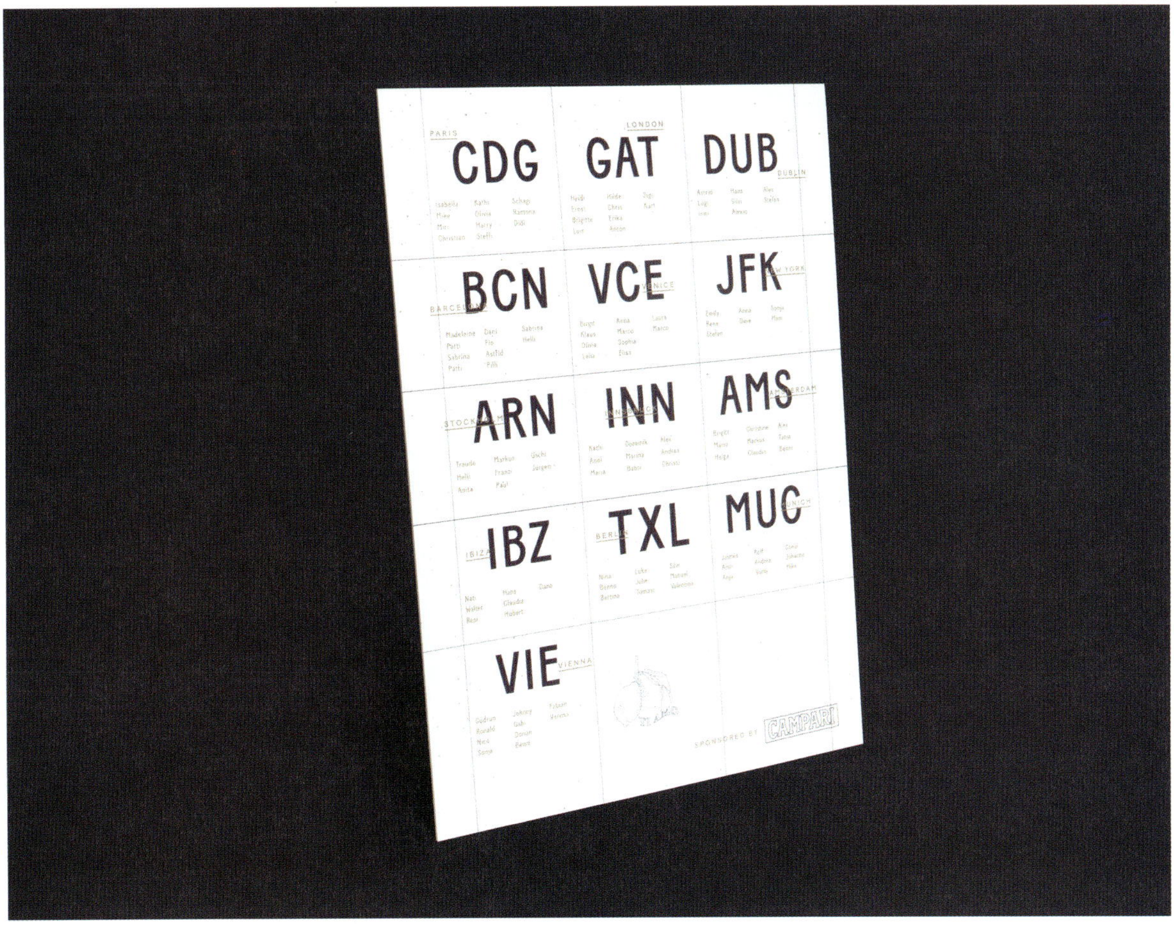

Marion and Darren's
Wedding Invitation

✉

Design Agency: Allons-y Alonso
Art Direction and Design: Audrey Colombié
Printing: Badcass
Client: Marion and Darren

Marion and Darren, a French couple living in Paris, decided to gather their loved ones and get married in Capri, Italy. Audrey Colombié created a wedding suite that became the guide to their journey. The program, which looked like a passport, was actually a folded, hand-drawn map with all the details of the wedding. The passport-like appearance was achieved by a golden hot foil printing on thick blue paper. The cards inside were printed on embossed 500gsm cotton paper.

DESTINATION
CAPRI

L° 24' 05" N   14° 12' 42" E

NAPOLI

• Napoli Capodichino (NAP)

Molo Beverello •   • Calata Porta di Massa

GOLFO
DI NAPOLI

POSITANO
×

SORRENTO

CAPRI
×

NOTA BENE :
A boat will ferry you
to and from Capri to Positano
for the wedding ceremony

ANACAPRI

Ricevimento
al Riccio

× Brunch
alla Villa Leone

CAPRI

Porto di
MARINA GRANDE

À VOUS

NON

NTS

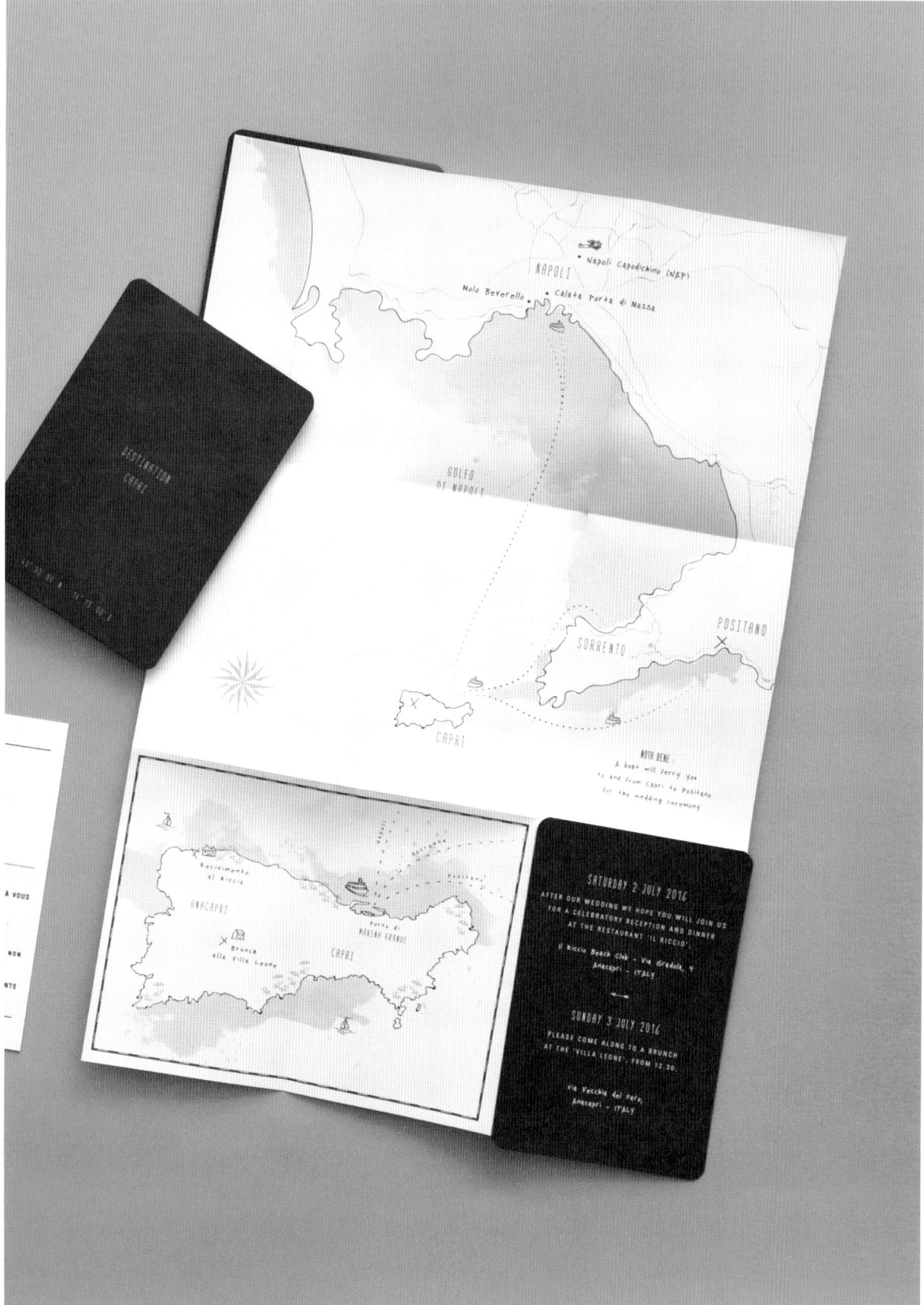

SATURDAY 2 JULY 2016
AFTER OUR WEDDING WE HOPE YOU WILL JOIN US
FOR A CELEBRATORY RECEPTION AND DINNER
AT THE RESTAURANT 'IL RICCIO'

Il Riccio Beach Club - Via Gradola, 4
Anacapri - ITALY

←

SUNDAY 3 JULY 2016
PLEASE COME ALONG TO A BRUNCH
AT THE 'VILLA LEONE', FROM 12.30.

Via Vecchia del Faro,
Anacapri - ITALY

Karine and Antoine's Wedding Invitation

✉

Design Agency: Allons-y Alonso
Art Direction, Design and Printing:
Audrey Colombié
Photography: Audrey Colombié

Audrey Colombié designed the wedding invitation for Karine and Antoine. Inspired by the location of their wedding, the birthplace of the French poet Jean de la Fontaine whose main works are fables with animals as characters, Audrey created the invitation with the couple's own tale—the love story of a rabbit and a fox. Each animal was hand-drawn in an engraving style. The invitation was printed on natural white 300gsm paper and the reply card, on thin silver vellum paper. The envelope was printed on 125gsm paper and folded by hand.

Souad and Sylvain's Wedding Invitation

✉

Design Agency: Allons-y Alonso
Art Direction and Design: Audrey Colombié
Client: Souad and Sylvain
Photography: Audrey Colombié

The guests of Souad and Sylvain's wedding were the lucky recipients of a golden ticket. Inspired by Willy Wonka's entry ticket to his chocolate factory, this invitation was printed on thin gold metallic paper from Arjowiggins' Curious Collection. What's more, an envelope with a hand-drawn map printed inside gave more details on the location of the wedding—like a treasure map.

DOSMILDIVUIT

✉

Design Agency, Art Direction and Creative
Direction: Partee
Client: El Gravat
Photography: Partee

This invitation was designed for the announcement of a New Year's Eve dinner at El Gravat, a restaurant in Barcelona, Spain. In this case, Partee arranged the typographical composition of DOSMILDIVUIT, which means "2018" in Catalan, and put the sherbet, a fizzy powder sweet—instead of cocaine—into little plastic bags that complemented the New Year's Eve dinner's menu.

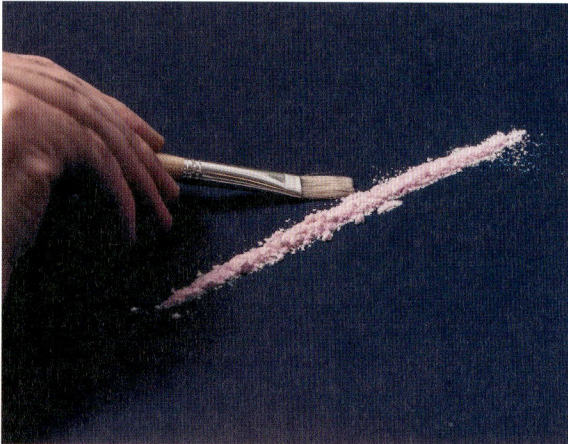

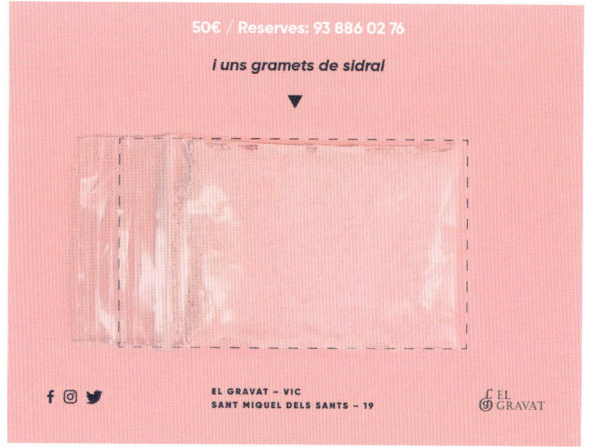

50€ / Reserves: 93 886 02 76

i uns gramets de sidral

▼

EL GRAVAT – VIC
SANT MIQUEL DELS SANTS – 19

EL GRAVAT

KBF 2016 S/S "LANDSCAPE" Invitation

✉

Design: Hiroe Nakamura
Client: URBAN RESEARCH co., Ltd.

The theme for KBF's 2016 S/S Collection was "LANDSCAPE." In this case, "LANDSCAPE" means the space from a certain point of view. Hiroe Nakamura used lines and geometric forms to express such a concept. And the green circular object is a fragrance tag. When the guests received this invitation, they could feel, smell and see the theme.

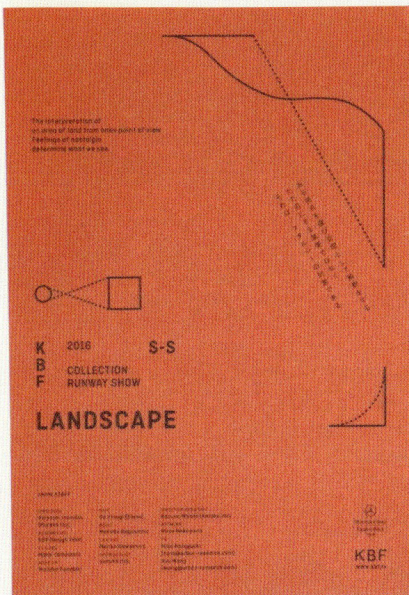

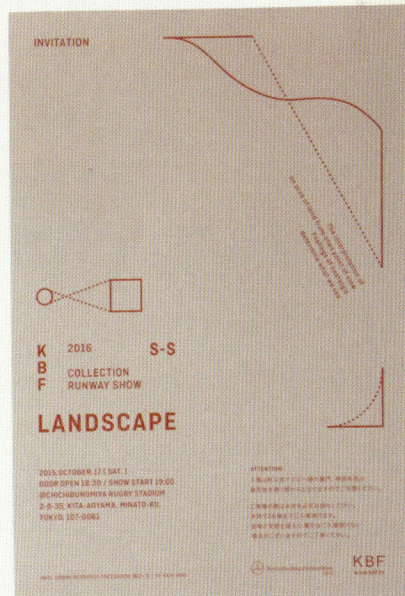

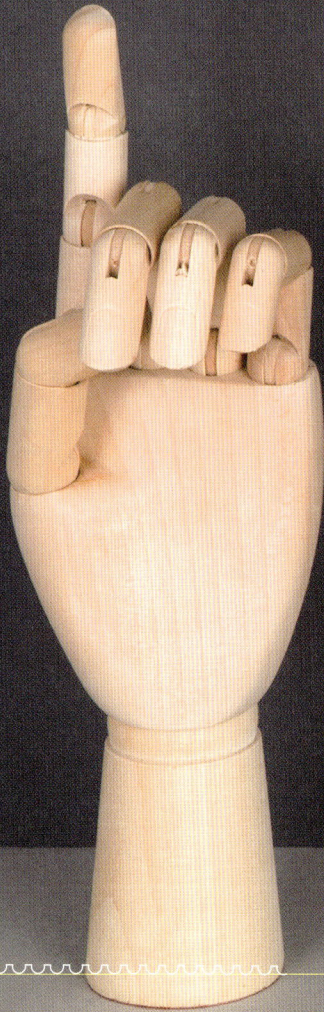

Machine Series
Greeting Cards

✉

Art Direction, Creative Direction, Illustration
and Design: Mayra Monobe
Photography: Las Coleccionistas

Inspired by the childhood games and
Rube Goldberg's inventions, this series
of five letterpress A6 cards tell different
stories, each ending with a fun greeting
for the recipient.

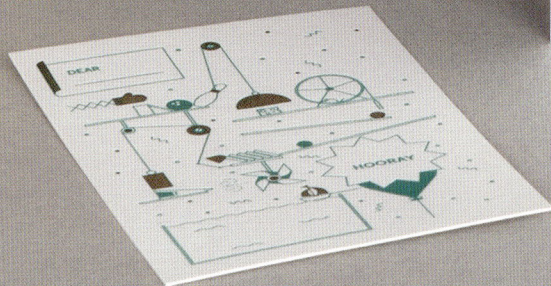

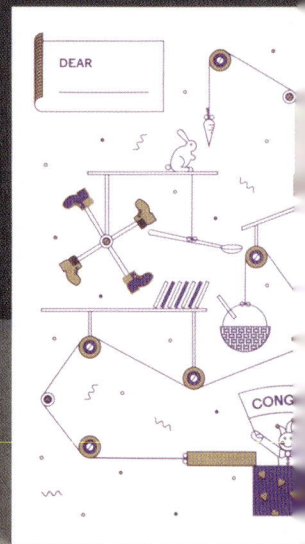

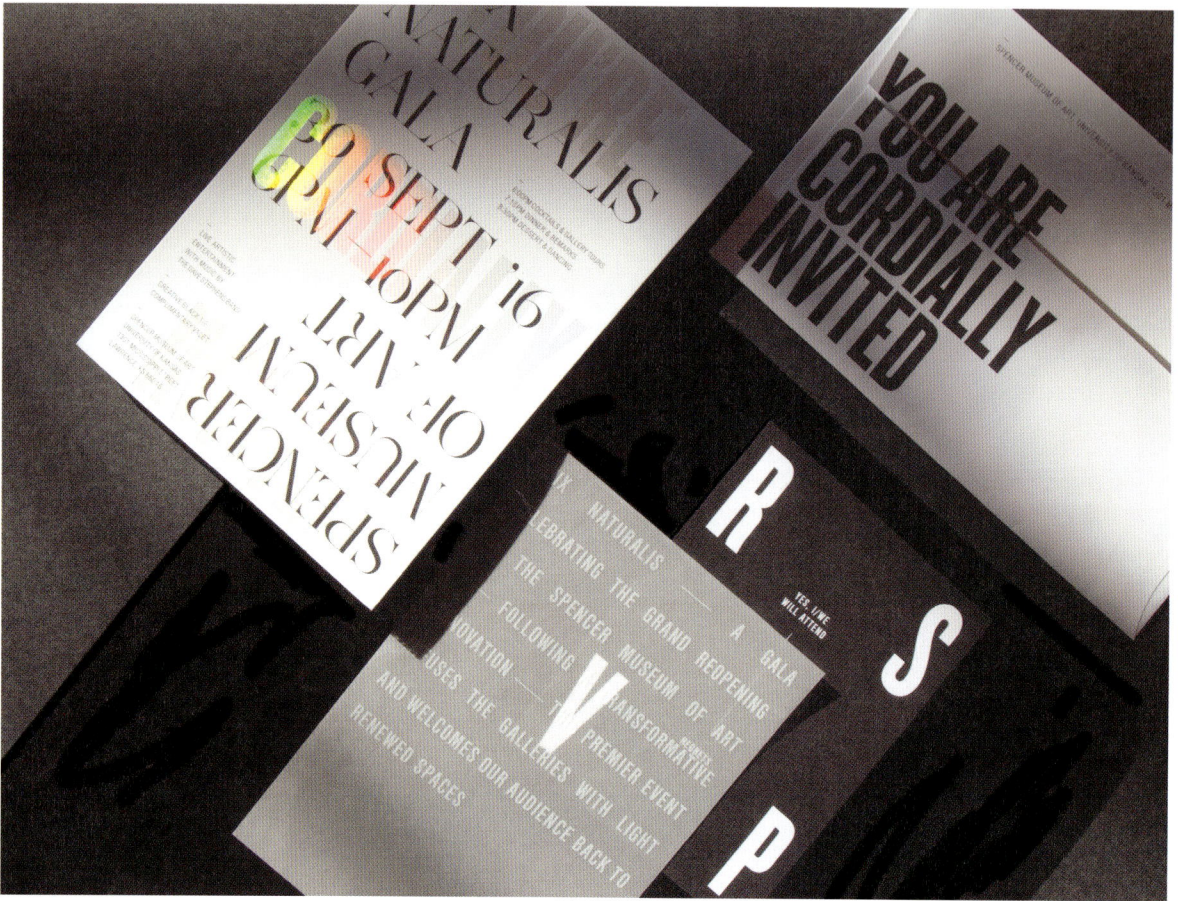

Lux Naturalis Gala Invitation

✉

Design Agency: Design Ranch
Creative Direction: Michelle Sonderegger and Ingred Sidie
Design: Rachel Roth
Client: Spencer Museum of Art

After major renovations, the Spencer Museum of
Art hosted a grand re-opening gala—Lux Naturalis.
Inspired by the introduction of natural light into
the space, an invitation was created to reflect the
transformed experience. Unique processes and paper,
kinetic typography and a clear holographic foil on the
invite as well as gala materials encouraged invitees to
experience the invitation in a new light.

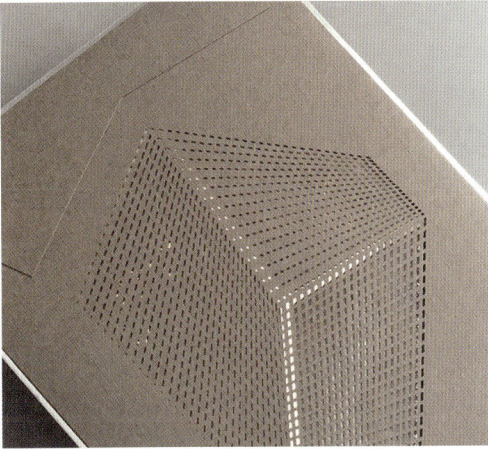

Sonderegger Luxepack
2017

✉

Design Agency: ENZED
Art Direction and Design: Mélanie and Nicolas Zentner
Printing: Sonderegger AG

Luxepack is an annual fair representing all aspects of packaging in the luxury industry. And Sonderegger is a factory specialized in laser cut, hot foil, embossing, micro-embossing and so on. The idea behind this invitation was to make a reference to packaging as a 3D object, but only using 2D techniques. The layered paper and tracing paper give the shape a depth and volume. What's more, the envelope shows some of the techniques mastered by Sonderegger, such as hot foil on the edge of a customized envelope and laser cutting.

Panka and Andris

⊠

Art Direction and Graphic
Design: SUBMACHINE
Printing: UNI Creative (Silkscreen)
and TCN (Laser Cutting)
Client: Panka and Andris

SUBMACHINE designed several
wedding invitations for their friends,
Panka and Andris. The components
of these playful invitations can be
assembled into a bunny and a bear
who represent Panka and Andris.

Erdei Buli

2017 szeptember 23.
Lósi Major
Veröce, Lósi völgy út 1.

Örömmel értesítünk, hogy
minden bátorságunkat
összeszedve, szeptember
23-án házasságot kötünk.
Szeretnénk, ha osztozn
velünk e nap örömeiben
ezért szeretettel várunk
ezen a szép őszi napon.

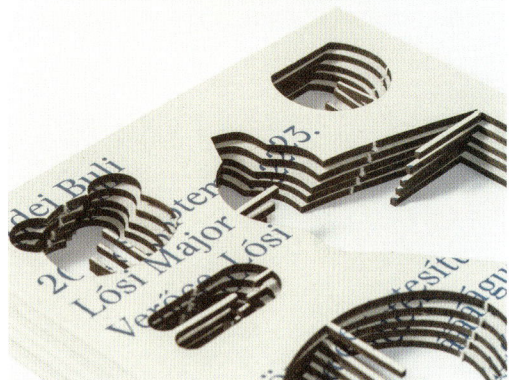

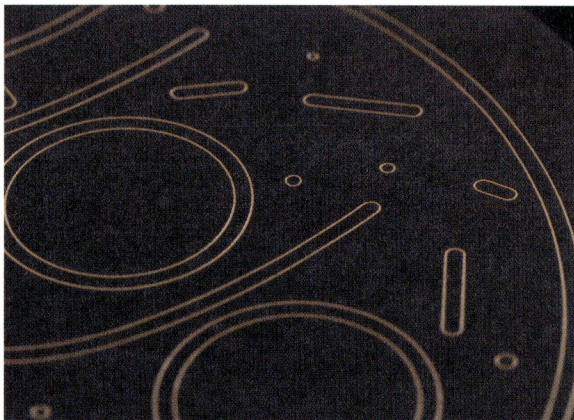

Christine's Bride Cake Wedding Invitation

✉

Design Agency: StudioPros
Art Direction and Design: Yi-Hsuan Li
Photography: Shengyuan Hsu

This invitation is a blessing the designer gave to her friend, Christine, for her wedding and it's a delicate design representing completeness and perfection, different from common, rectangular invitations. This invitation is shaped like a bride cake, a traditional cake given in East Asian cultures, and the structure of the key visual, the Chinese character xi (happiness), follows the same circular shape—smooth and sleek. The designer also quoted the line—"So they are no longer two, but one flesh (Matthew 19:6)", on the edge of the invitation to make a finishing touch.

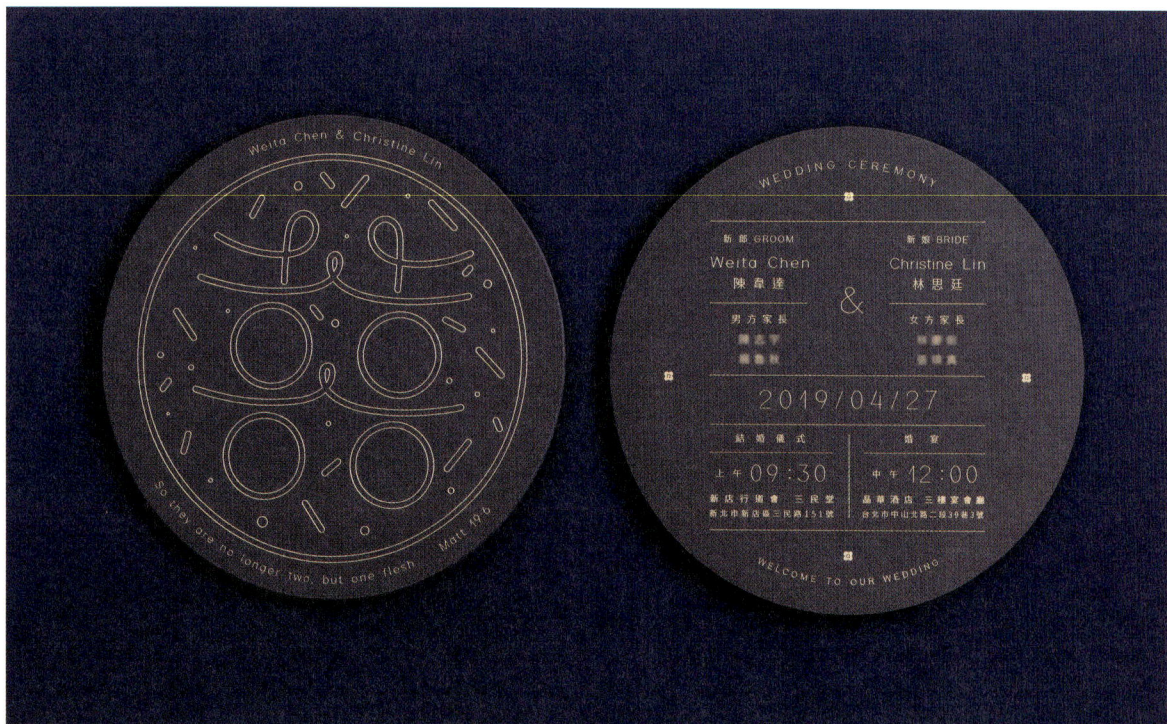

Love Facts

✉

Design: Meng Zhang
Client: B&M
Photography: Ethan Li

Each couple has its own love story,
anniversaries and meaningful dates that
signify every stage of their relationship.
The 600gsm thick grange paper board
with laser foil stamps marks those
important dates in their relationship. The
visual symbols, such as the Chinese
zodiac and the years of birth, are
deliberately scattered around the canvas.
In addition, there is an attached wishing
card where guests can write their good
wishes and blessings to the couple.

Our Wedding (Eszter and Miklos 18.08.2018)

✉

Design: kissmiklos
Photography: Eszter Sarah and Kevin Harald Campean

The design of this project was based on some manipulations of famous classic paintings. The faces on these iconic paintings were changed to Eszter and Miklos'. They designed postcards like souvenirs in a museum shop and made invitations for their family and friends that looked like exhibition invitations. Also, they printed the paintings on canvas in their original size and organized a real exhibition before the wedding.

o-apartamento
Invitation Card

✉

Design Agency: MUSA WORKLAB

For their new office's opening, MUSA
WORKLAB designed an invitation
that celebrates the occurrence and
development of life events in a happy and
beneficial way surrounded by the natural
environment.

O Apartamento tem muito gosto em convidar

para o cocktail de inauguração do seu novo
espaço, quarta-feira 24 de outubro,
as 18h30.

Largo de São Mamede 4 e 5, R/c
1250-236 Lisboa

DJ Set by Yen Sung

o-apartamento

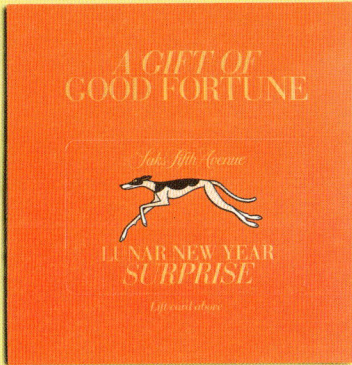

Invitation and Gift Card for Saks Fifth Avenue

✉

Design Agency: Studio-Takeuma
Design Direction: Joy Szilagyi
Illustration and Typography Design:
Studio-Takeuma
Graphic Design: Lauren Crooks
Client: Saks Fifth Avenue

This invitation and gift card was designed for the lunar new year 2018. Since the year 2018 was the year of the dog in the Chinese zodiac, the invitation set brings good luck, elegance and a powerful visual hierarchy.

Xu and Wang's
Wedding Invitation

✉

Design Agency: SIWEI DESIGN
Creative Direction: Si Wei Lai
Client: Xu and Wang
Photography: Maybe Chang

SIWEI DESIGN created this wedding
invitation for Xu and Wang. To represent
the blessings to the couple tying the knot,
SIWEI DESIGN specially designed a logo
on the wedding invitation, which signifies
the wedding ring and holding hands.

Ethan and Ashely
Wedding Invitation

✉

Design: Sion Hsu
Client: Ethan Lee
Photography: Ethan Lee

Sion Hsu designed this wedding invitation with folded sheets. Because a wedding basically means combining two families, Sion used tree branches and flowers as visual elements to form a new family tree. After the main visual was decided, Sion used a leather string to tie the four cards together. Sion also selected different colors to show both tradition and fashion.

S&Y Dream Home
Wedding Invitation

✉

Illustration and Design: Dyin Li
Client: S&Y
Photography: ChenYu Ho

Longing and dreaming for their future
family, the new couple feels warm and
comfortable in the romance of their
wedding. This wedding invitation,
designed with the concept of dream
home, shares with their guests their
home, ideals and daily life. A key inside is
decorated with the couple's intials.

正因為我們都不完美
我們才會彼此需要

World Partner Forum - Bordeaux

✉

Design Agency: Paperlux Studio
Creative Direction: Max Kuehne
Client: Daimler Financial Services
Photography: Tom Medici

Paperlux Studio created the motto—
"Deeply Rooted"—for the World Partner
Forum 2018 in Bordeaux and enjoyed
developing the corporate design for
this event. The graphic elements on the
stationery were hand-written or hand-
drawn. The invitation is a flip-box where
someone can turn the wheel to reveal the
venue of the forum for that year.

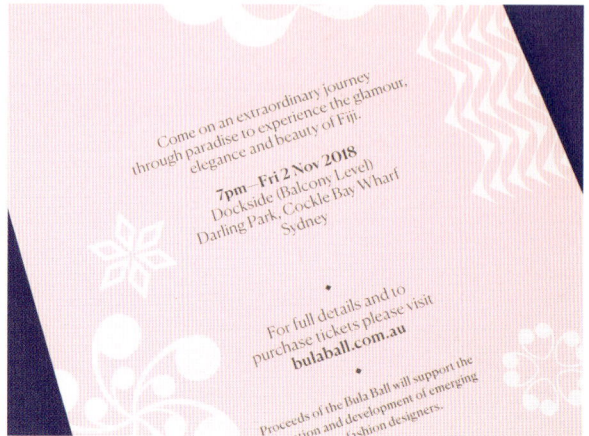

Bula Ball

✉

Design Agency: Strategy Creative
Design: Geoff Courtman and Kevin Teh

This premium printed invitation was part of the brand identity of an inaugural fundraising gala for the nonprofit Fijian Fashion Foundation, called the Bula Ball. Bula means "life" and "hello" in Fijian. The designers focused on the idea of tropical glamour. They created an elegant stencil display font with an accompanying series of ornaments and patterns. The invitation was printed on duplexed Colorplan cardstock with white and black ink.

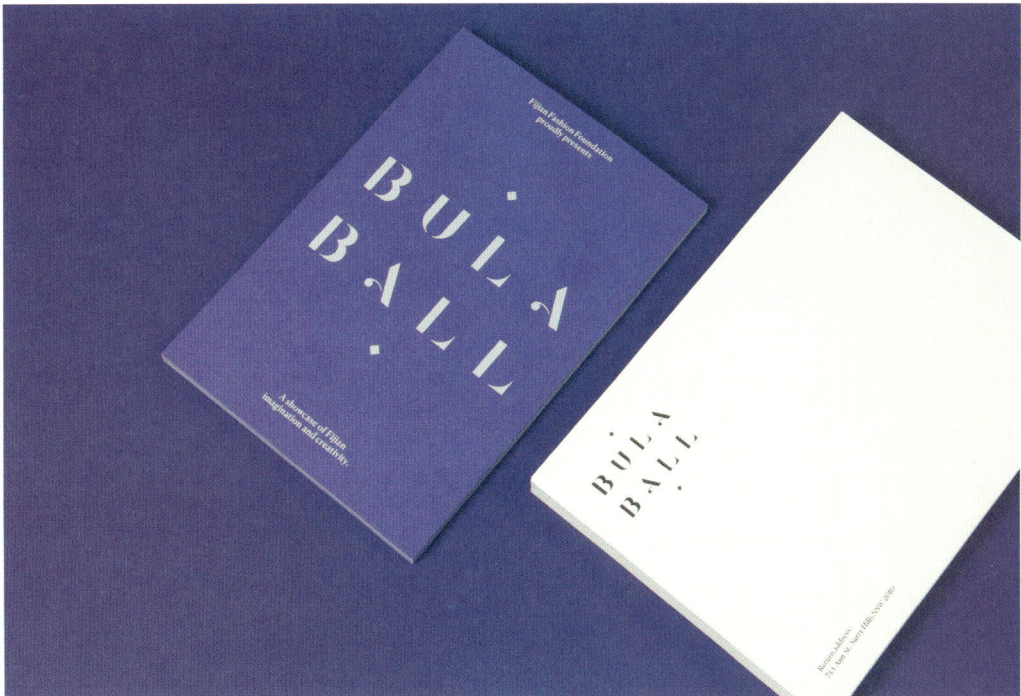

D&J Wedding Card

✉

Design: Sean Huang
Client: D&J

Sean Huang got inspired by the clients' love stories. He chose several keywords and symbols from their stories, such as adventure and travel, to use on the invitation card. The main visual is a Canadian mountain against a starry night illustrated with two zodiac signs, which were meaningful to the clients. The backside with relevant information is also a simple night sky and mountain.

Go forward for 10950 Days, then Turn Left

✉

Illustration: Ino Lai
Design: Sion Hsu
Client: Ino Lai
Photography: Ben Chen

''Go forward for 10950 Days, then Turn Left'' was the second chapter of Ino Lai's solo exhibition in The Factory-Mojocoffee. The designer extended the Chinese character xiang (forward) to surround the ''10950 days.'' A lot of images and words overlap and echo the accumulation from the ages. Meanwhile, the matte gold was used to display Ino Lai's typography.

D&R Wedding Card

✉

Design: Sean Huang
Client: D&R

There is a retro-style illustration showcasing the combination of the bride's and groom's Chinese zodiac (monkey and rooster) and astrological signs (Aries and Libra) in this customized invitation card. The ribbon in the shape of an infinity symbol shows their eternal love. Distinctive from traditional wedding invitations, this design has a strong visual impact with its combination of eastern and western influences. The quality bright-colored paper was chosen and treated by hot stamping. Sean Huang hopes that recipients feel impressed and special.

7 Katowice
JazzArt Festival

✉

Design: Marta Gawin

The shape of the trumpet is the main
inspiration for this visual identity.
Meanwhile, the festival's name and the
relation between the instruments and
the festival's motto are the main two
typographic designs.

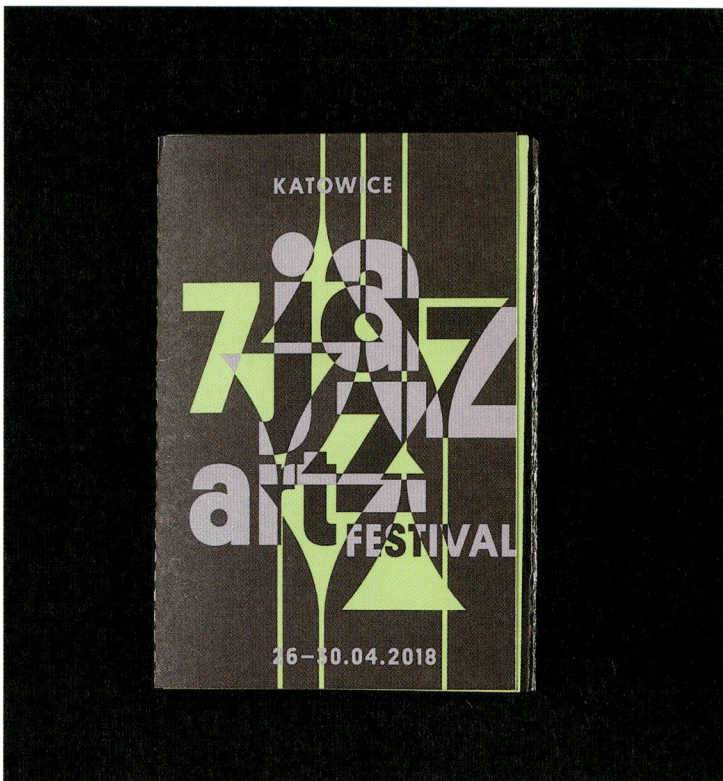

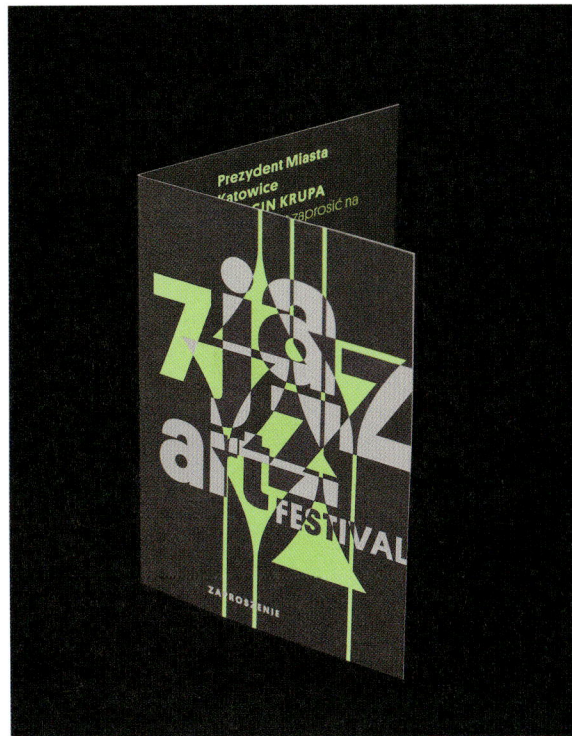

L&J Wedding Card

✉

Design: Sean Huang
Client: L&J

Sean Huang used the irregular particles and rough surface of gray, recycled, thick paper to simulate the texture of stone. By using the embossing effect, several hollows and grains on the paper looked like weathered rock, which reflects the concept of eternity in this wedding card. The exposed gold and natural minerals with golden and laser stamping effects represent rarity and preciousness as time goes by. And the fossils of shells and leaves symbolize everlasting love.

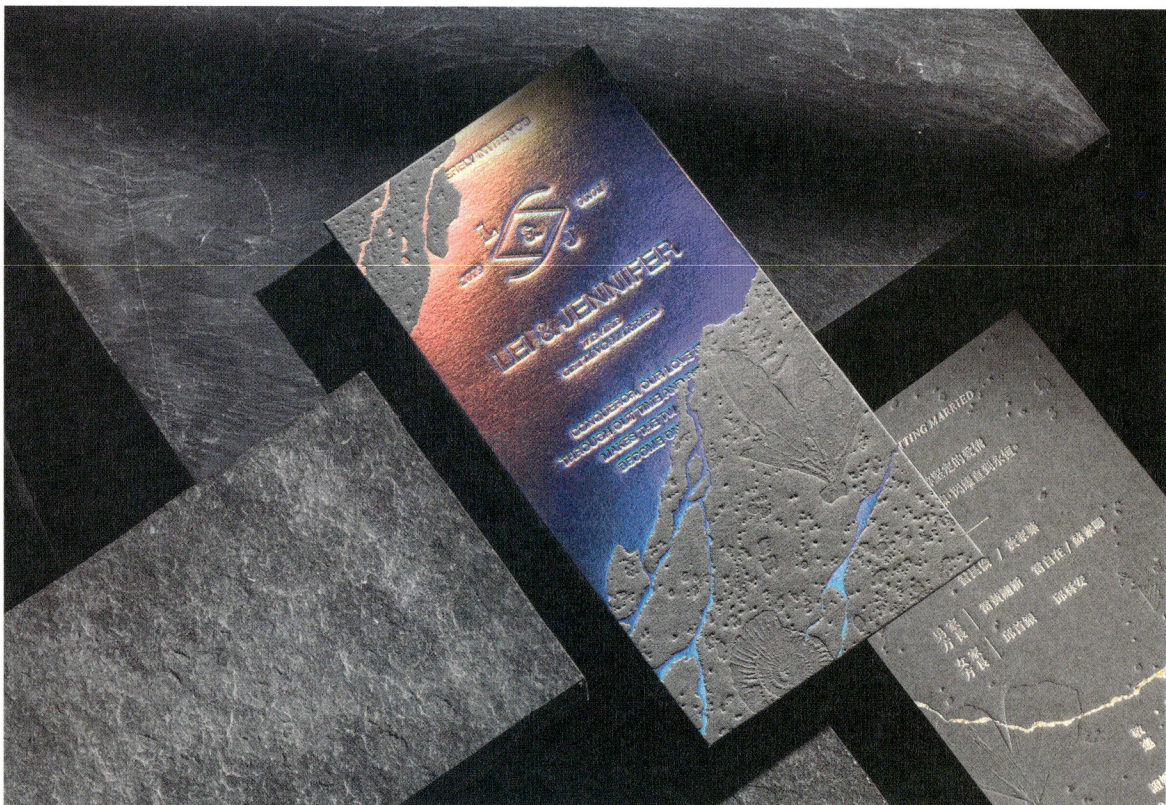

dotdotdot *Kurzfilmfestival* Wien
Filmscreening und Nachgespräche
2.Juli – 23. August 2019
jeden Donnerstag und Freitag

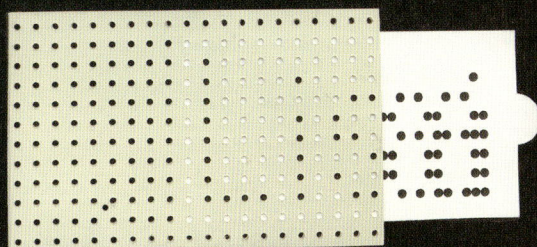

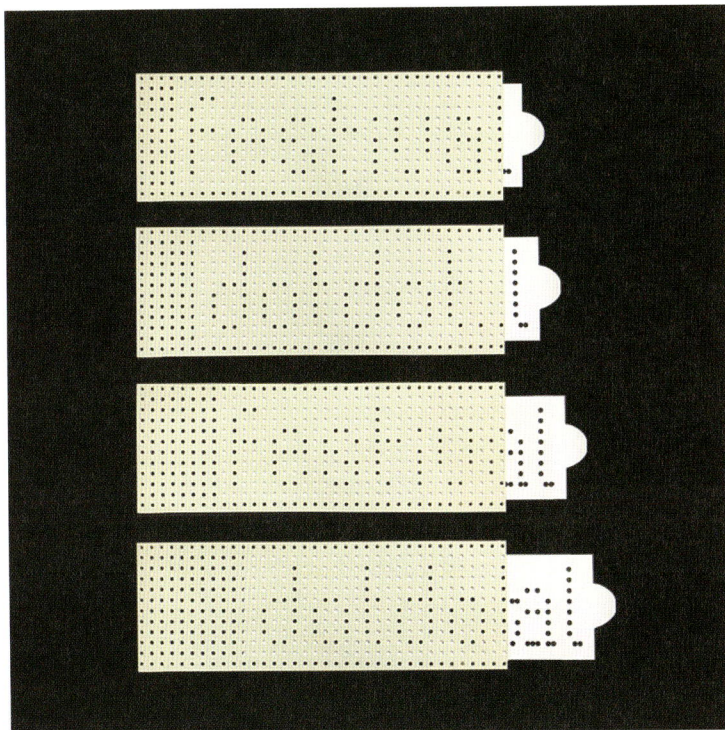

dotdotdot Festival Card

✉

Design Agency: soju.studio
Art Direction: Selin Göksu
Client: dotdotdot Film Festival

The dotdotdot Film Festival asked soju.
studio to design an invitation card. soju.
studio took a more interactive approach
to the card's design and designed it to
function as a film festival ticket. With the
information regarding the film festival on
it, this "ticket" is an exclusive greeting
card for the sponsors and special guests.

Cherish Box and
Wedding Invitation Pack

✉

Design Agency: (shame-on-you)office
Printing: SENSIN Packaging
Client: Arthur and Anna
Photography: (shame-on-you)office

The project is a bespoke wedding cherish box and invitation pack for the newlywed couple, Arthur and Anna. The cherish box features a drawer opening with a built-in ribbon handle for the guests to carry easily and the inner box has a tailored ethylene-vinyl acetate foam lining with suede coating. The invitation pack consists of a nude color ribbon-tied envelope, a semi-transparent topographic map and a burgundy gold foil stamped bilingual invitation.

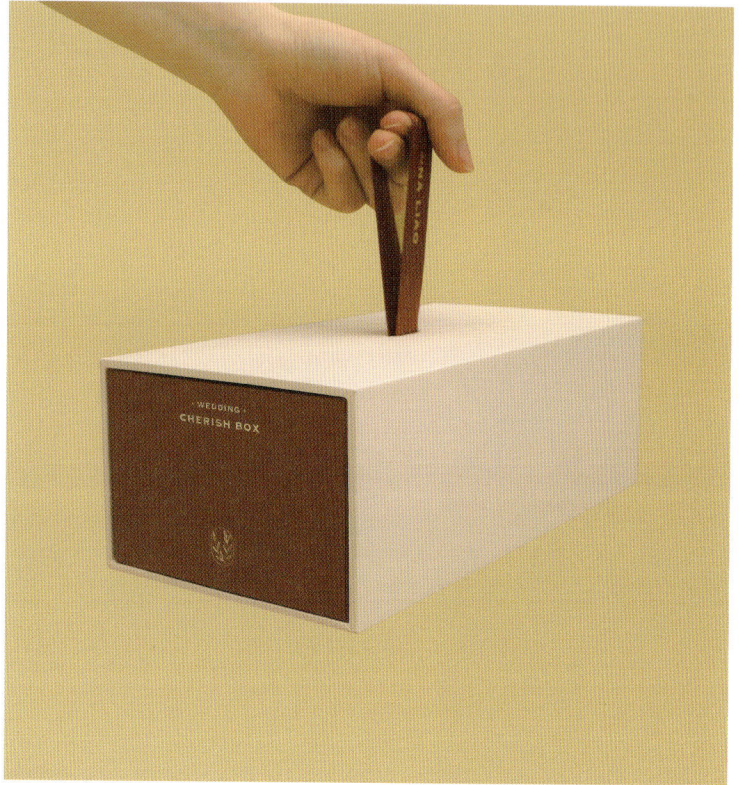

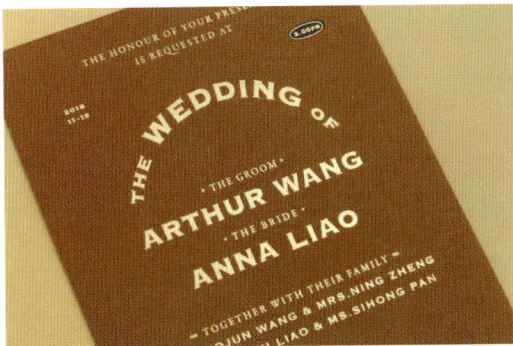

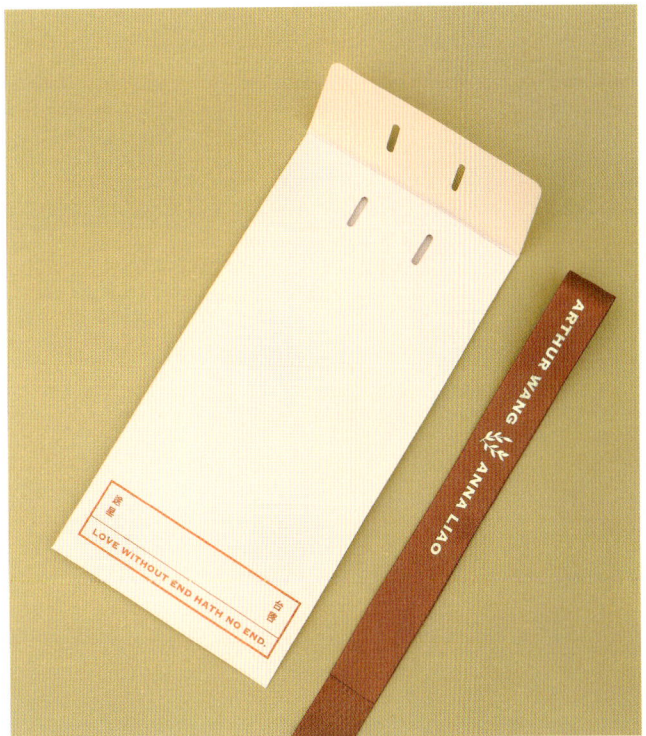

Love and Marriage

✉

Design: Dan Elliott
Client: Talia and Daniel
Photography: Mark Lobo

Dan Elliott designed a set of wedding
collateral based loosely on the notion of
great combinations—cheese and wine,
love and marriage, and Talia and Daniel.
The imagery, paper stock, finishing
and color palette all pay homage to
the wedding venue Glasshaus.

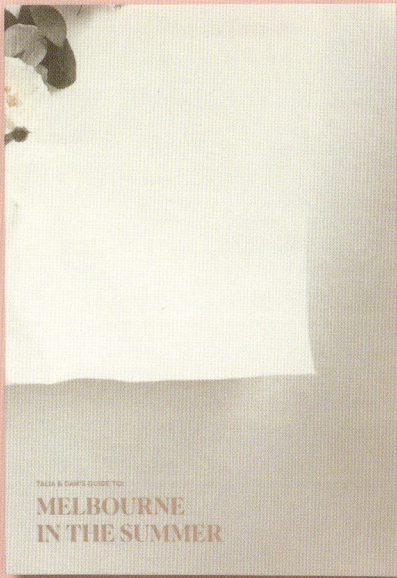

TALIA & DAN'S GUIDE TO:

**MELBOURNE
IN THE SUMMER**

Our wedding would not have
been the same without you.
We're truly grateful for your
presence on our special day.

**LOVE &
THANKS**

**TALIA &
DANIEL**

XIẾC 2019

✉

Design: Lam Thao

XIẾC is an annual international circus festival in Vietnam for children from five to 12 years old. The artwork focuses on the smoothness and rhythm of each design with different shapes. The illustrations display the circus artists' movement. The rugged, but simple brushstrokes with contrasting colors show the overall vigor. Moreover, the innovative magic box is foldable. The transparent glass box can help the viewers see everything inside clearly and evoke interesting experiences.

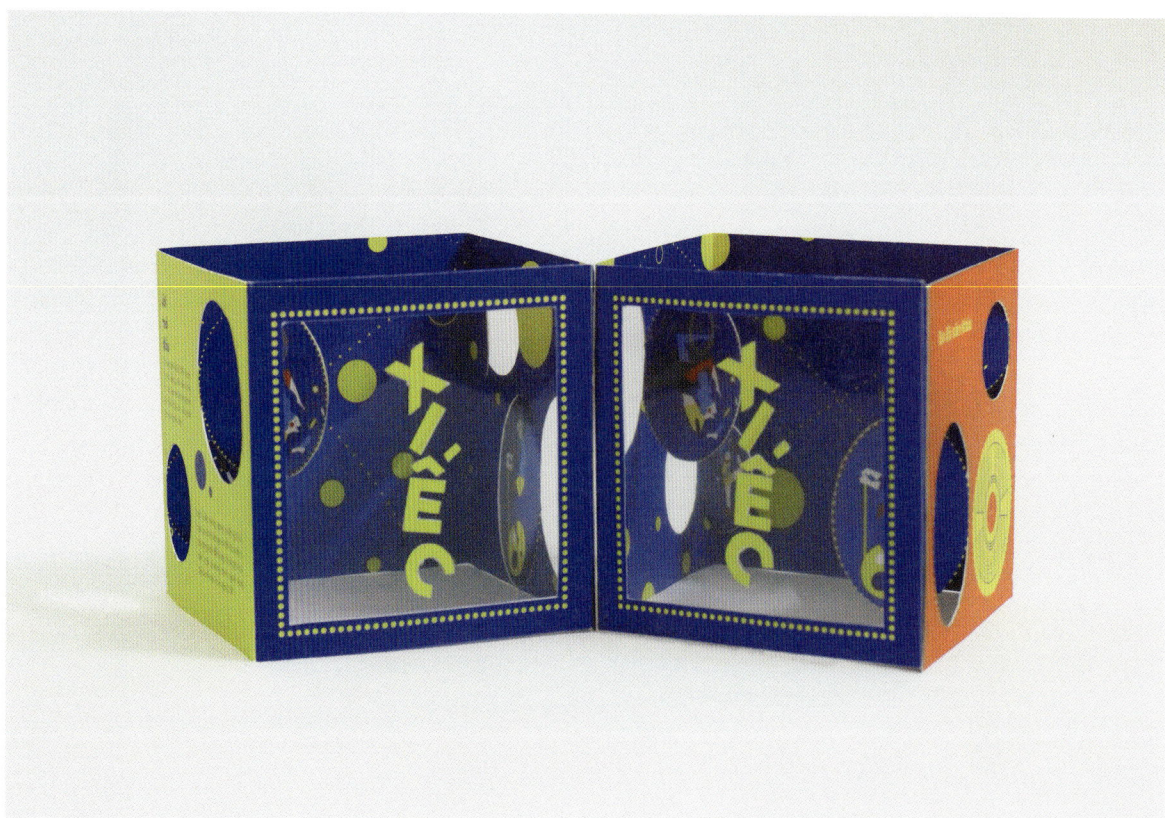

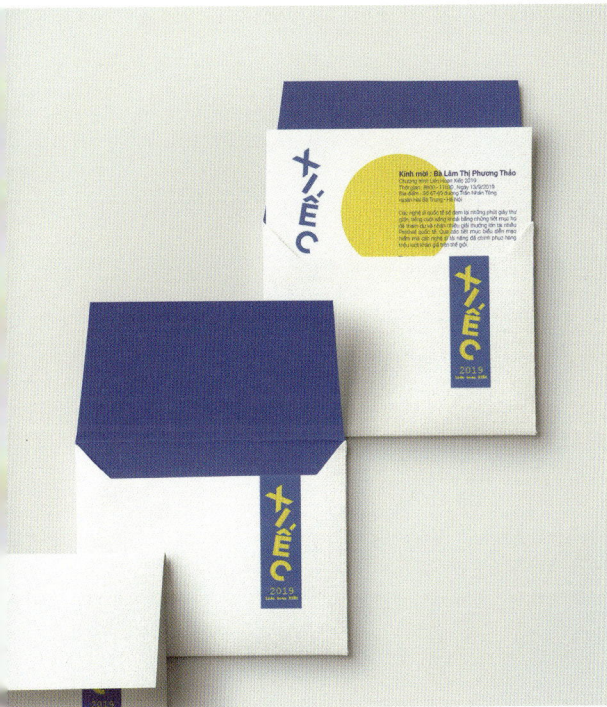

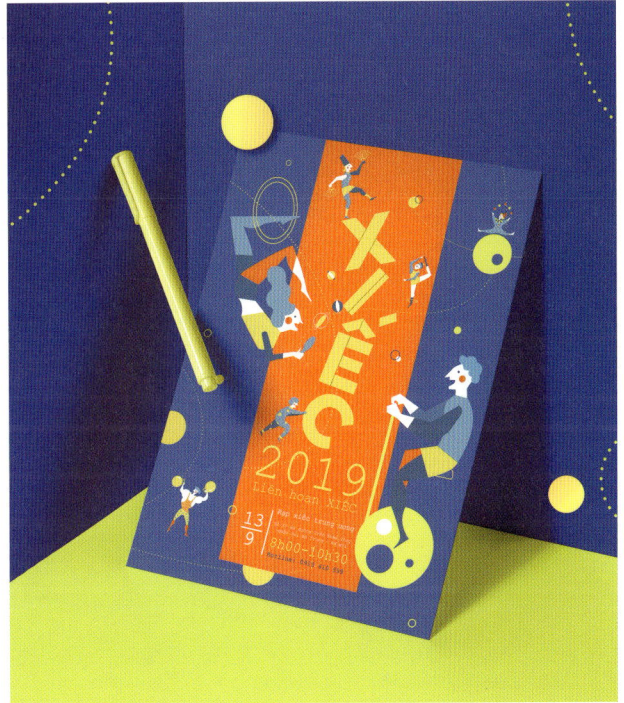

Sestra Store Opening Invitation

✉

Creative Direction and Design: Kristina Bartošová
Copywriting and Cooperation: Thomas Pokorn
Printing: Infinitive Factory
Client: Sestra Store
Photography: LippZahnschirm

The concept store of Sestra in Graz, Austria, is full of
playful fashion and accessories. To match the vibe
of the brand, Kristina Bartošová created a beautiful
invitation to the store's opening. The typography on
the invitation is a custom-made typeface for this brand,
printed on a piece of luxurious paper, Gmund Action
in Pastel Heart Attack color. The paper has a unique
honeycomb structure and is complemented by bright
pink, metallic, hot foil stamping. With the blind-
embossed envelopes and holographic wrapping, the
invitation represents charm and luxury.

Cresa 30th Anniversary Invitation

✉

Design Agency: Taylor Design Works
Creative Direction: Matthew Taylor
Design: Allison Flores Goebel and
Matthew Taylor
Printing: Modern Press
Client: Cresa

To announce the 30th anniversary celebration of Cresa, Taylor Design Works created this invitation card. With the use of die-cut and holographic foil, this invitation card reminds the recipients of confetti and fireworks.

Jonathan and Emma Star Book Wedding Invitation

✉

Illustration and Design: Dyin Li
Client: Jonathan and Emma
Photography: ChenYu Ho

Responding to the wedding theme, Dyin Li made a star-shaped wedding invitation. When the recipient opens and fully expands the invitation, it becomes a star consisting of a story in infinite loops.

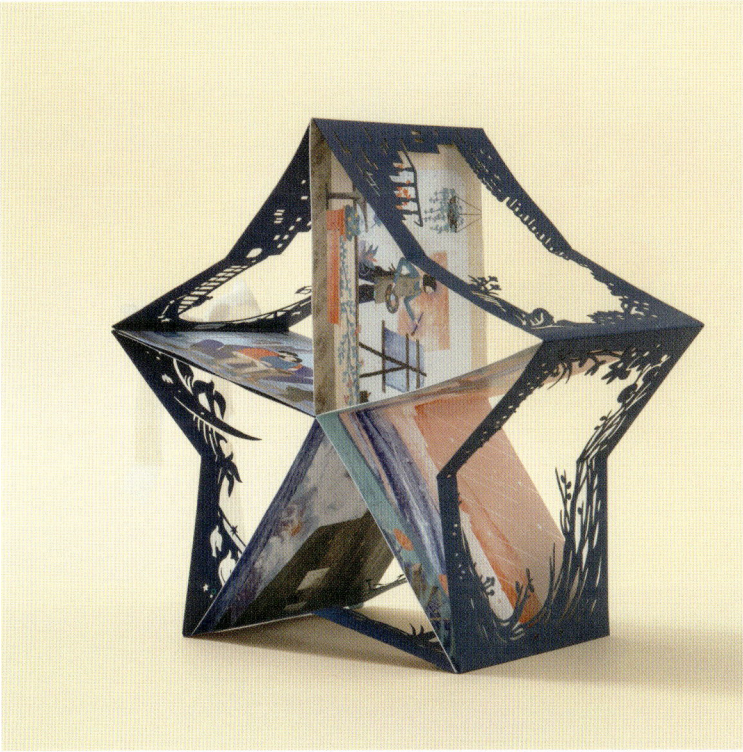

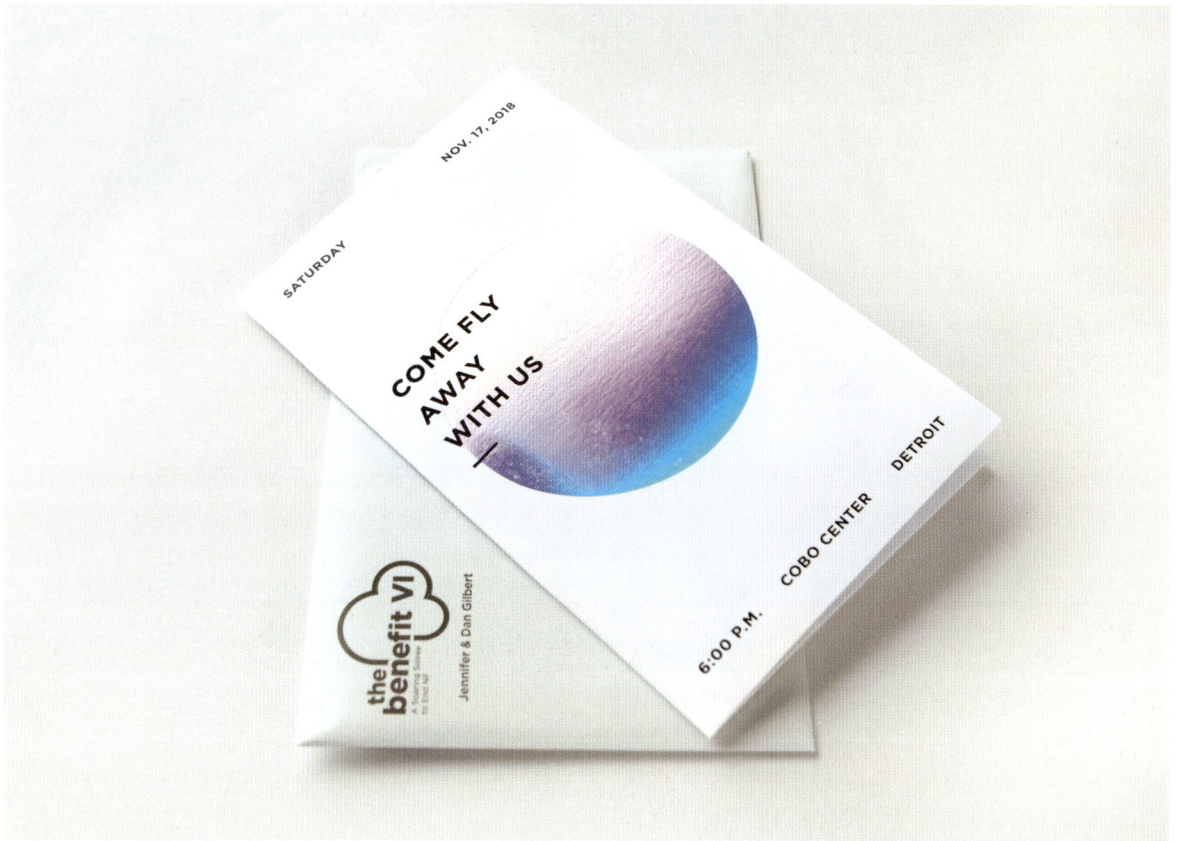

NF Gala 2018 Invitation

✉

Design Agency: Quicken Loans Creative Team
Design: Sarah Fogel and Allison McGinn

NF Forward is an organization for raising funds and awareness for a rare genetic disease called neurofibromatosis. Quicken Loans Creative Team partnered with the nonprofit to create an invitation suite for the 6th annual gala. The team set "The Sky's the Limit" as the invitation's theme and pushed beyond expectations and reached higher to work toward the goal of NF.

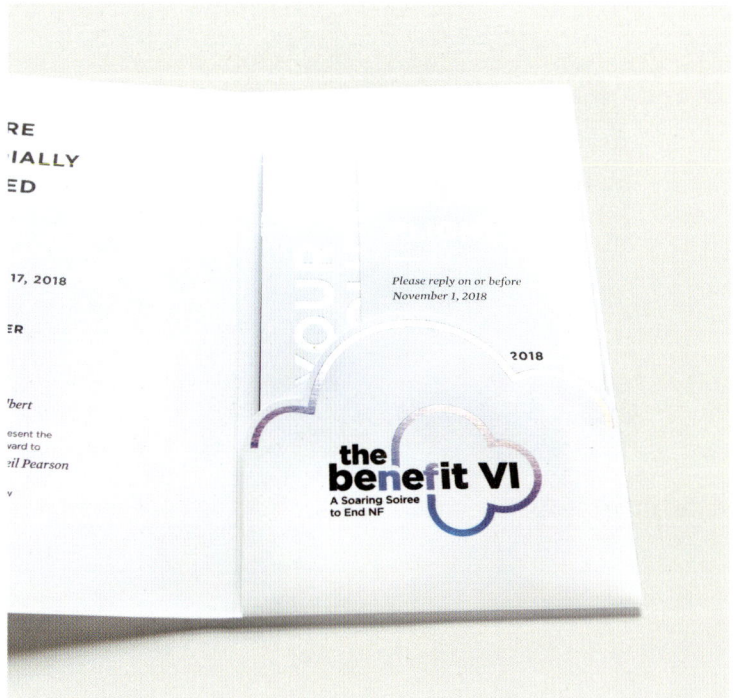

LOCATION

Cobo Center
1 Washington Boulevard
Detroit

PARKING

Complimentary valet parking
will be available at the Cobo
Center entrance located on
Washington Boulevard at the
corner of Jefferson Avenue,
near the Cobo Center marquee.

HOTEL

For your convenience,
a block of rooms has
been reserved at:

Greektown Casino-Hotel

1200 St. Antoine
Detroit, MI 48226
(877) 424-5554
bit.ly/2KT5HLs

(Hotel URL is case sensitive.)

PLOT YOUR COURSE

Honorary Committee
as of August 24, 2018

RESERVE YOUR FLIGHT

Please reply on or before
November 1, 2018

**SATURDAY
NOVEMBER 17, 2018
6:00 P.M.
COBO CEN**

SHINING

Our sincerest
thanks for
your incredible
generosity!

Honorary Committee
as of August 24, 2018

OUR SHINING STARS

The Run To Monaco

✉

Design: Why
Creative Direction: James Kent
Client: The Run To

The Run To is a five-day supercar rally that takes place every summer. Inspired by the golden age of GT motoring, the 2019 run was from Paris to Monaco with good food, fine wines and five-star hotels along the way. This invitation was sent to an exclusive group of high net worth individuals around the world. The invitation was screen-printed in gold on walnut to echo the Belle Époque in Paris. And the route information was printed on Colorplan in gold and printed on a sleeve embossed with the logo of the event.

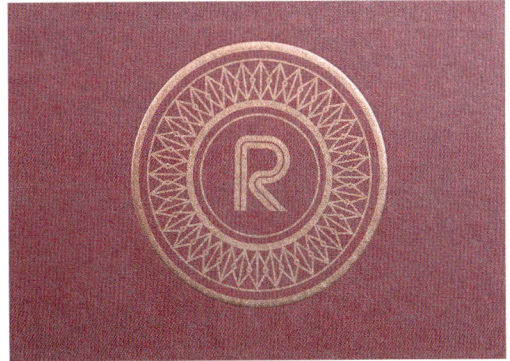

50 Years of National Archives of Singapore Film Screening

✉

Design Agency: The Workbench
Art Direction: Ella Zheng
Creative Direction: Ryan Len
Client: National Archives of Singapore
Photography: Aureate

The designers segmented the different pages into categories and bound them together into a flyer. Besides using a stately deep green and accents of metallic copper to anchor the overall theme of these films about stability and progress, complimentary warm colors, such as beige and pink, were also introduced to liven up the cheerful and community-driven narratives of other chosen films. As an extension to the private screening, the VIP program sheet can also be bound together easily, ensuring consistency in design direction.

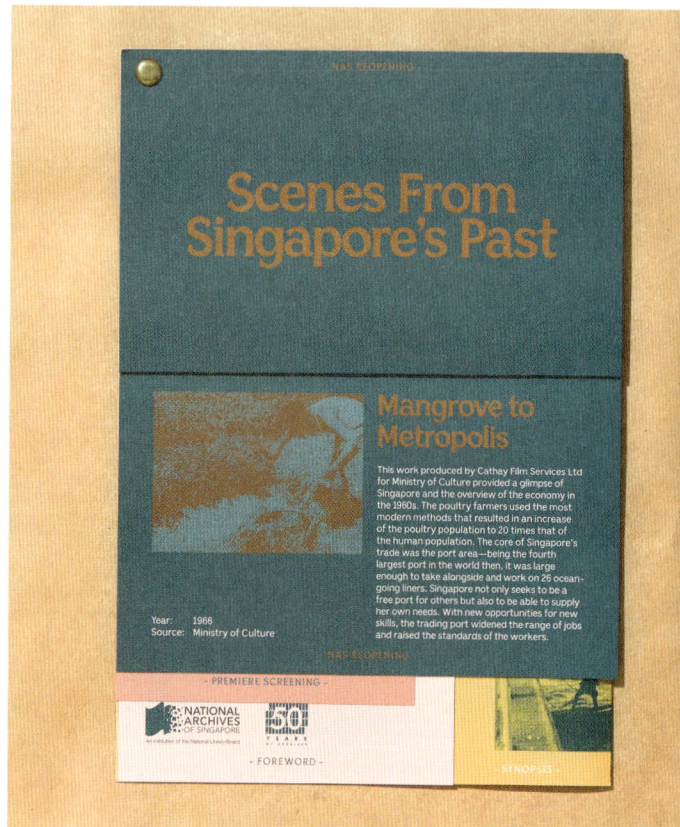

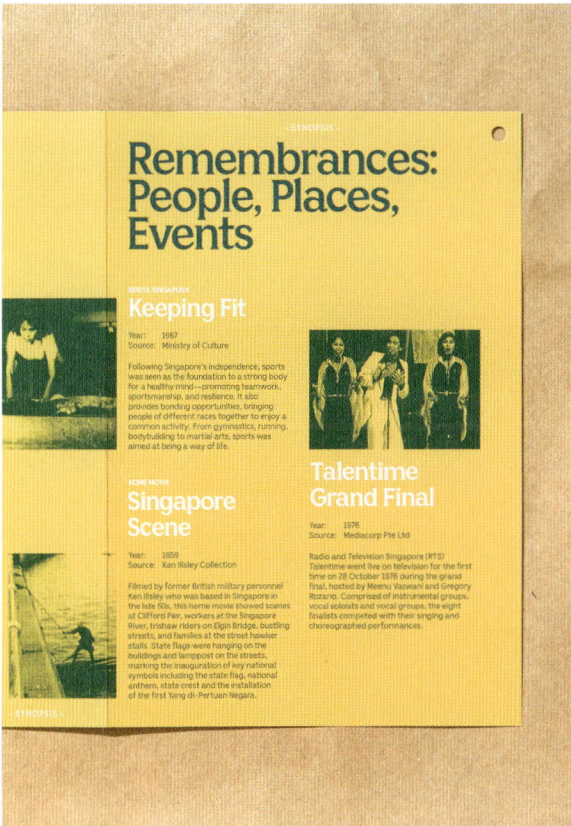

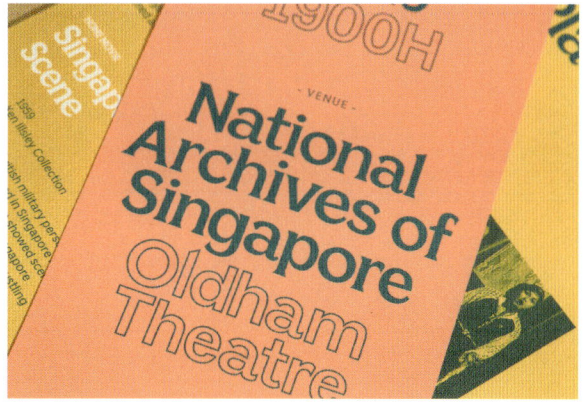

Intertwined in Holy Matrimony

✉

Design Agency: The Workbench
Art Direction: Ella Zheng
Creative Direction: Ryan Len
Client: Renny and Charlynne
Photography: Aureate

The word "intertwine" is defined as "to be very closely connected with something or somebody else." And this became the inspiration for the monogram. The initials of the couple were intertwined to form a symbol, which represents the inseparable connection. The envelope holds both the church's and banquet's invitation cards. Taking a cue from Renny's Peranakan roots, the juxtaposition of the Peranakan-tiled backdrop against the simplicity and luxurious typographic card complements each other perfectly without being overly kitsch.

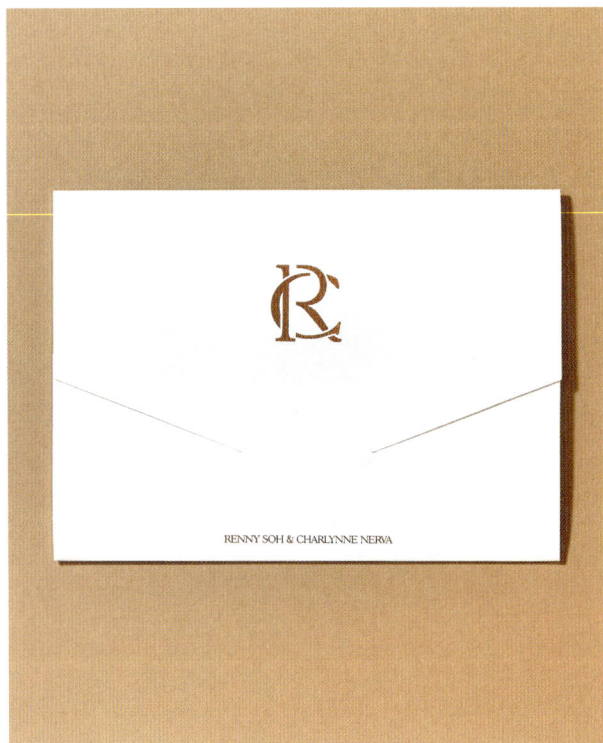

Together with their parents

Renny Soh
and
Charlynne Nerva

Warmly invite you to join them for the celebration of their marriage and an evening of merriment.

Venue:
The Fullerton Hotel
1 Fullerton Square
Singapore 049178

Time:
Saturday
5th October 2019
7.00 PM

Dress Code:
Black Tie

Charlynne Nerva

Warmly invite you to join them for the celebration of their marriage and an evening of merriment.

1 Fullerton S
Singapore 04

Time:
Saturday
5th Octo
7.00 PM

Dress Code:
Black Tie

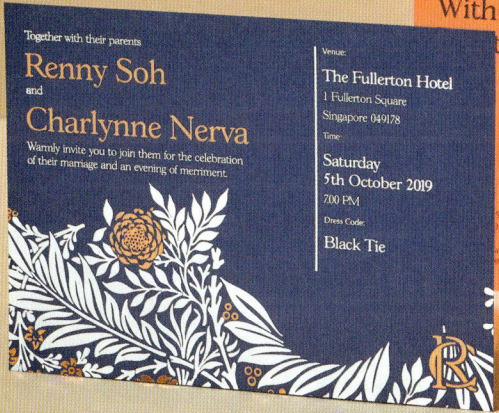

Kindly Respond
With Your RSVP
By 5th June 2019

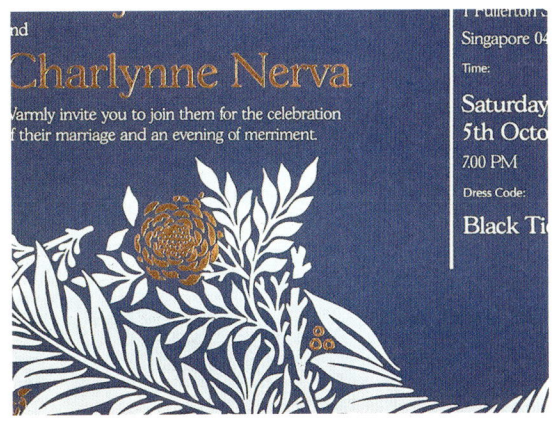

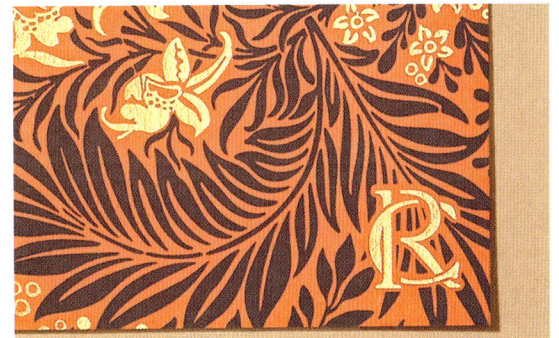

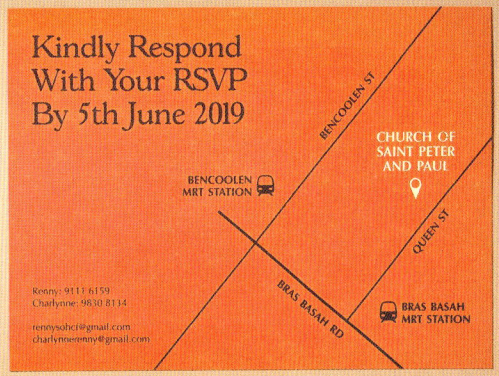

FULLERTON RD

ESPLANADE DR

THE
FULLERTON
HOTEL

BATTERY RD

FULLERTON RD

RAFFLES PLACE

Renny: 9111 6159
Charlynne: 9830 8134

rennysohcf@gmail.com
charlynnerenny@gmail.com

RAFFLES PLACE
MRT STATION

Kindly Respond
With Your RSVP
By 5th June 2019

BENCOOLEN ST

CHURCH OF
SAINT PETER
AND PAUL

BENCOOLEN
MRT STATION

QUEEN ST

BRAS BASAH RD

BRAS BASAH
MRT STATION

Renny: 9111 6159
Charlynne: 9830 8134

rennysohcf@gmail.com
charlynnerenny@gmail.com

Wedding Celebration of Ryan and Ella

✉

Design Agency: The Workbench
Art Direction: Ella Zheng
Creative Direction: Ryan Len
Client: Ryan and Ella
Photography: Aureate

Decorated in gold and white, the wedding of Ryan and Ella was full of a tropical island's temptations and celebratory vibes. The wedding invitation was illustrated and gold-foiled on a thick, cotton card stock. Each wedding favor was unique, featuring one photo each from their pre-wedding shoot, which encouraged the guests to share their slides around the table and create conversations. It also came with an enamel pin as an ode to their guests. Their engagement and wedding rings were also designed by the couple themselves.

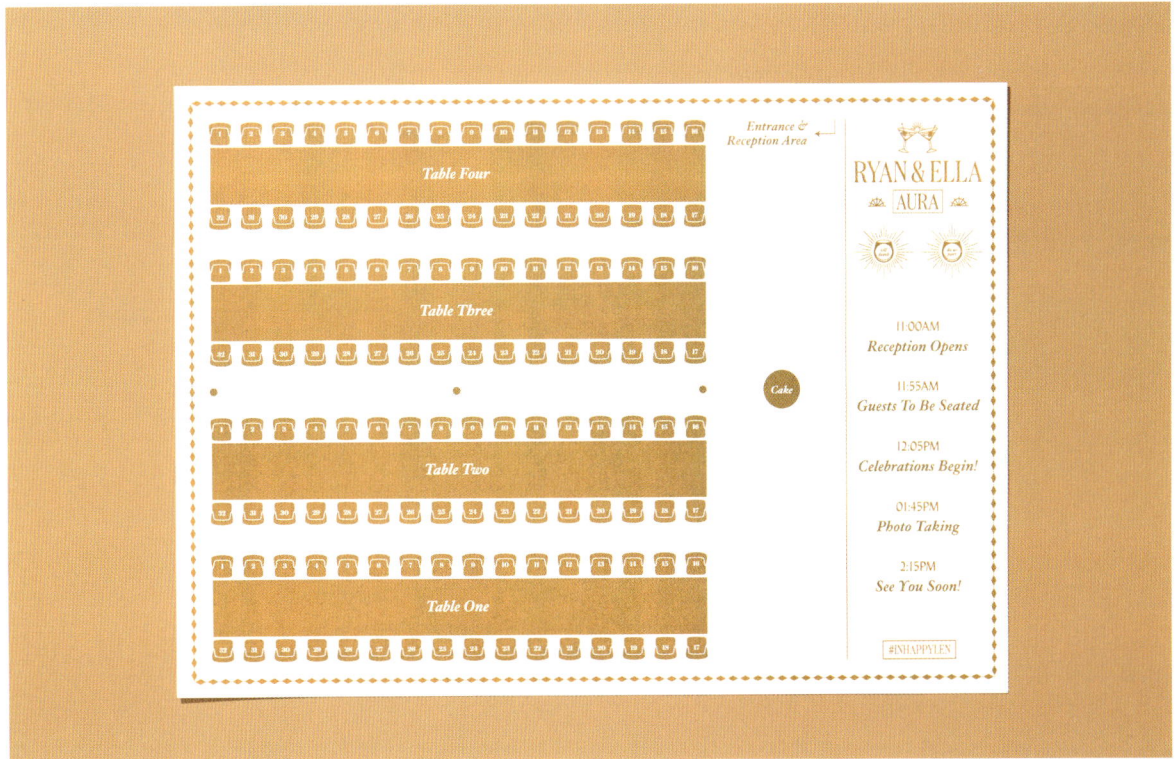

Moving Spaces

✉

Design: Evan Wijaya

This project is an exercise in playing with shapes, colors, motions and compositions for an exhibition held by a fictional interior design studio. The aim was to accomplish several graphic explorations and create a sense of space.

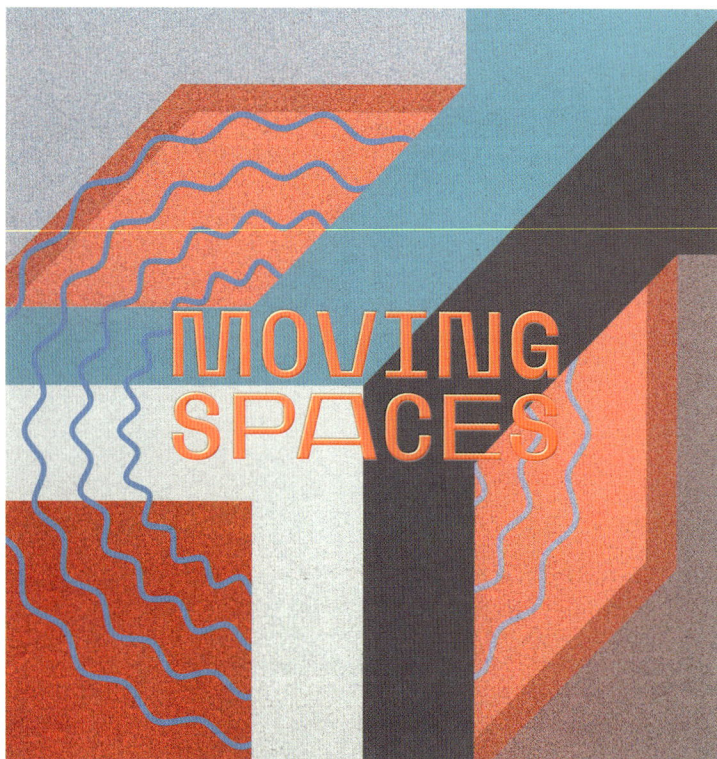

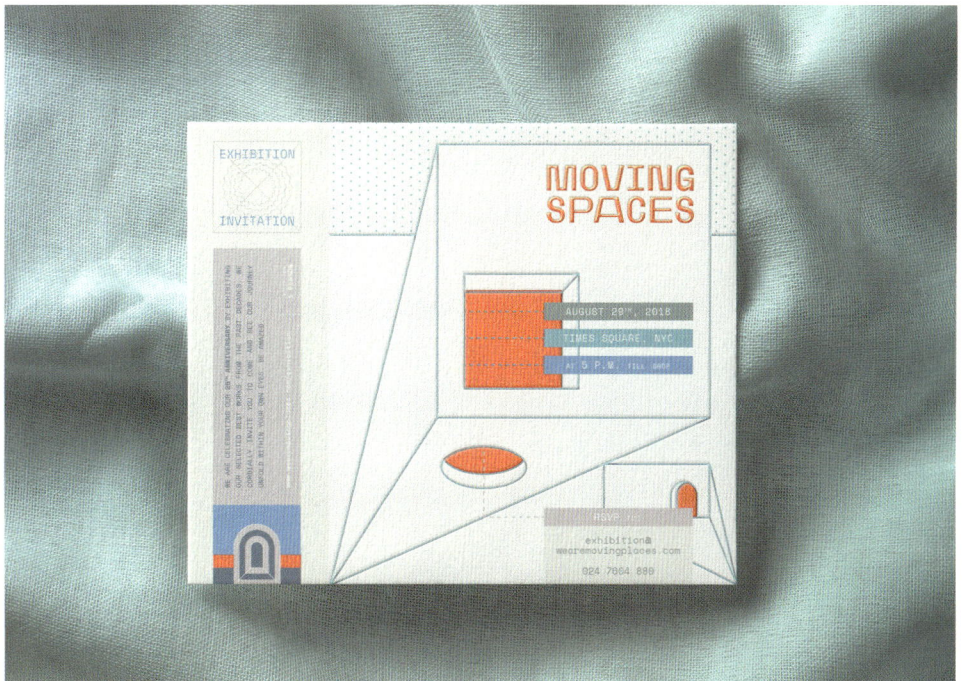

A-PO and Nancy

✉

Design: Siang-Hua Chang
Client: A-PO and Nancy

With the technology of plateless printing and gilding, Siang-Hua Chang designed this wedding invitation for a new couple. The couple met and fell in love during late-night hours. What's more, they complement one another. To highlight these, Chang used two different kinds of gold foil to form the round moon. The sea made by gilding symbolizes the harmony of marriage.

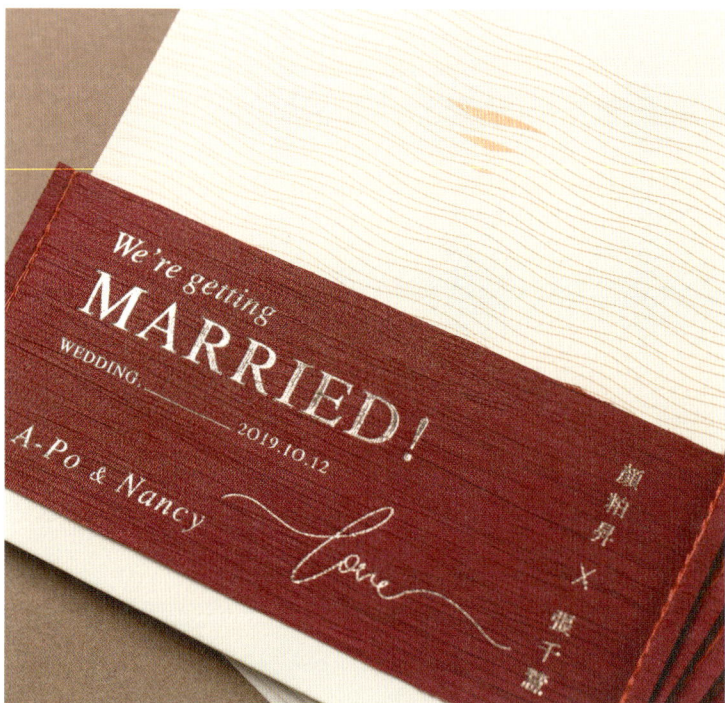

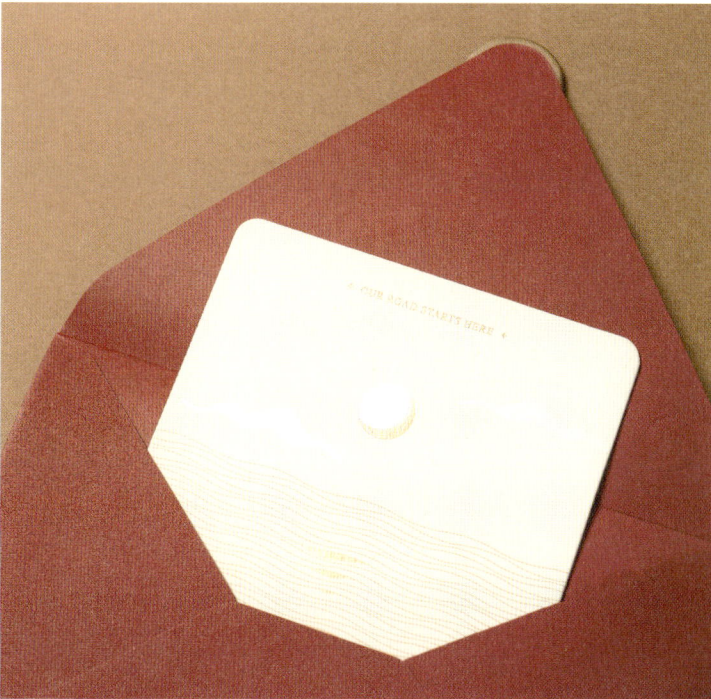

Evita Tsai and Tim Lin
Wedding Invitation

✉

Design Agency: Ti-Ming Chu Workshop
Printing: Tooget
Client: Evita Tsai and Tim Lin
Photography: Po-Chiao Huang

The cover of this wedding invitation consists of a Chinese herb, oroxylum indicum, which means "wooden butterfly." And it symbolizes the bridegroom's job and the meaning of love. The layout blended both Western and Chinese elements, such as the word "LIFE" formed by Chinese strokes. A coil of hemp rope surrounding the invitation represents the solid relationship of the new couple.

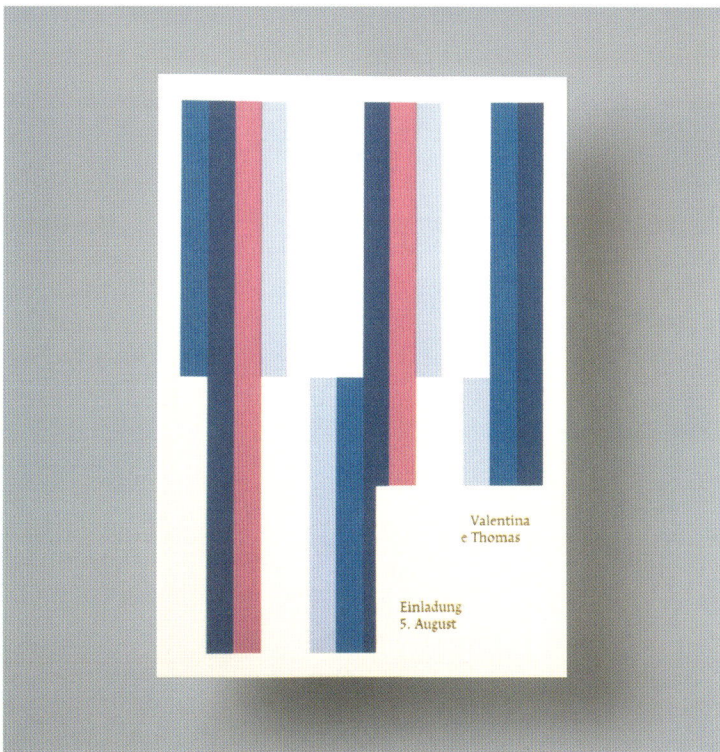

Bonfim Wedding

✉

Design Agency: Sunda Studio
Design: Susanne Bauer and Armin Reinhold
Client: Valentina and Thomas

For the wedding of Valentina and Thomas, two designers adapted the elements of Bonfim, the tradition Brazilian Bahia bands. They presented the marriage bond graphically in blue and pink, using various weaving, braiding and knotting techniques. The invitation adopted silkscreen with custom acrylic paint and gold embossing on Gmund cotton paper.

Anthology of an
Object Exhibition

✉

Design: Alexander Kuliev

Anthology of an Object is an exhibition
in Moscow Manege, which divides into
two parts representing the works of
two artists—Alexander Martitosov and
Vladimir Martirosov, a father and his
son. Alexander Kuliev tried to reflect the
contrasts between them. The invitation
consists of thick, uncoated paper with
letterpress and black-and-white photos
printed on tracing paper.

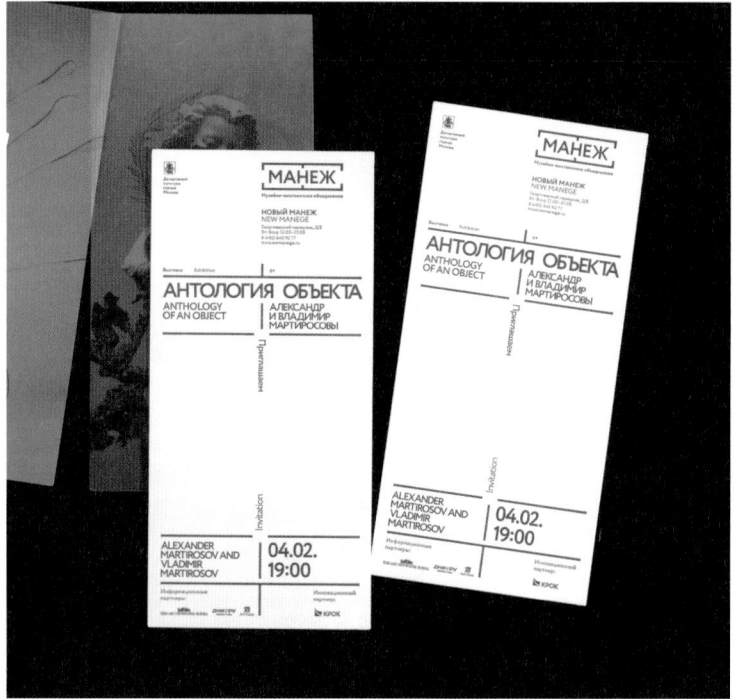

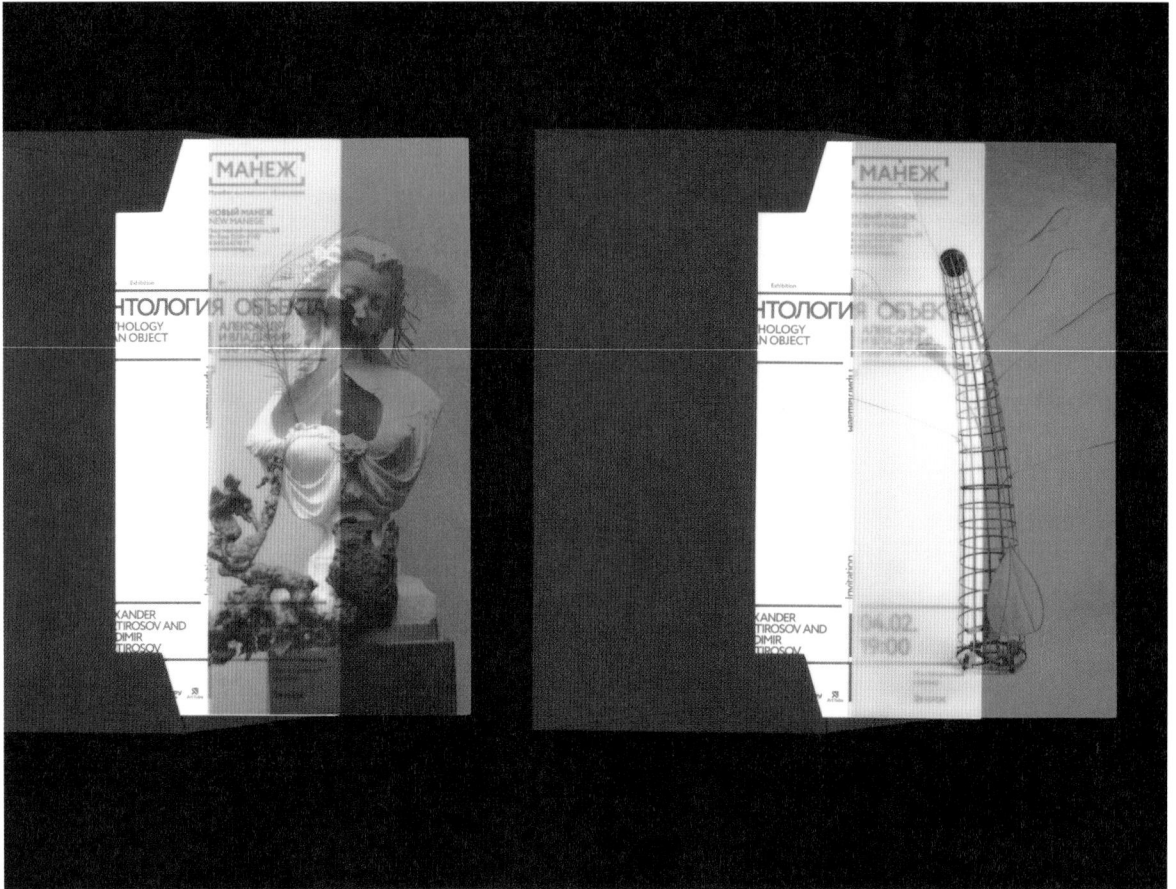

POSTCARDS

A postcard is a quick and easy way to stay in touch while traveling or to send a short message without needing an envelope. Despite a seemingly simple format — an illustration on one side, an address and blank space for writing on the other — the following designs are fun, unique and worth holding onto long after they've been received.

Wildcolor

Illustration and Design: Trongtran
Client: Indigo home
Photography: Trongtran

This postcard project was started when Trongtran moved to Da Lat, Vietnam to live and he was focused on naturally dyed fabric products. At first, the illustrations of the plants used for vegetable dyes were drawn for Trongtran's research and knowledge. Then Trongtran transformed the illustrations into an art publication that can provide a large audience with knowledge about the plants and dyeing fabric.

Afterthought
Postcard Series

Design: Olga Vasik
Client: Card Nest Ltd.
Photography: Card Nest Ltd.

Olga Vasik was commissioned by Card Nest, a greeting cards subscription service from Bristol, England, to create a postcard series called Afterthought. This series consists of six humor-filled postcards with a healthy dose of sarcasm in the form of an afterthought. Card Nest came up with messages for the cards and Olga created a mix visual design of lettering and illustrations.

I JUST Called TO SAY...

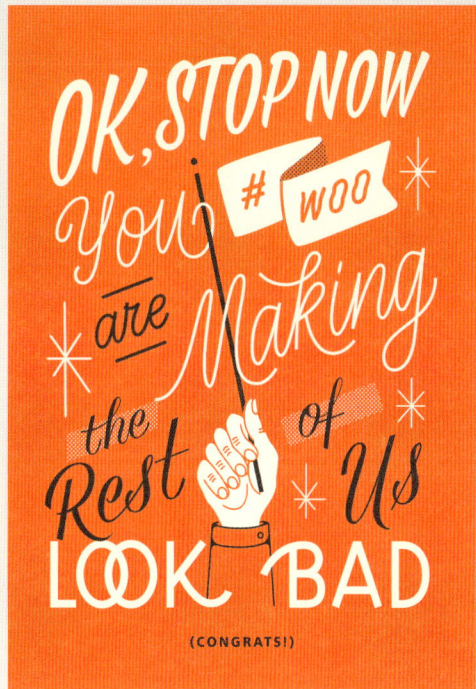

OK, STOP NOW YOU are Making the Rest #woo of Us LOOK BAD

(CONGRATS!)

I LOVE YOU More than Pizza

(BUT DON'T ASK ME TO PROVE IT*)

Happy Birthday SAUSAGE

(HOPE IT'S BANGIN')

Podarok #1

Design Agency: ESH gruppa
Illustration: Julia Popova, Natasha Dzhola,
Ksenia Turenko, Daria Litovchenko, Ivan
Tretyakov, Bela Unclecat, Stefan Lashko, Timur
Zima, Phillip Tretyakov, Valera Kozhanov, Mila
Silenina and Maria Yudina

Podarok (gift) is a printing project where
ESH gruppa and their friends make
postcards, stickers and other printing
materials. Podarok #1 issue is a set of
stickers and gift cards specially made for
the new year and Christmas holidays.

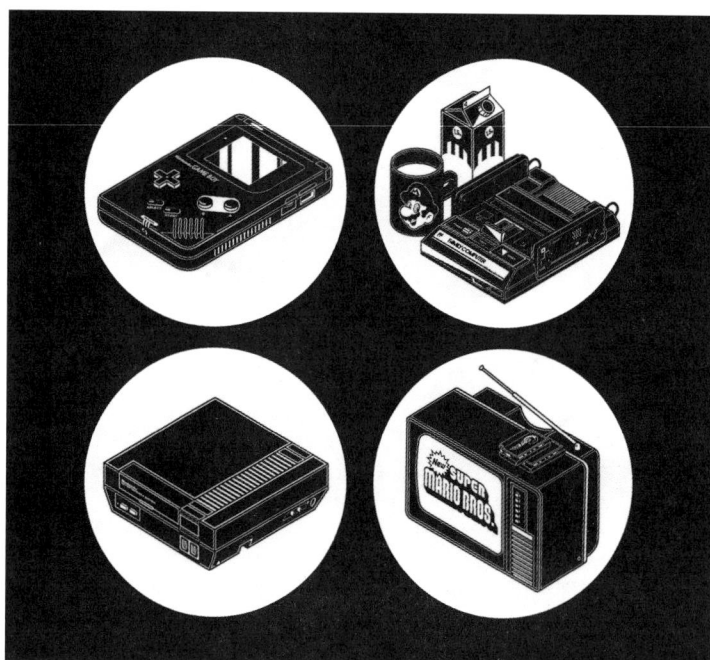

ПОДАРОК.

РУКОВОДСТВО ПАТИМЕЙКЕРА*
ПОДГОТОВЬ КОМНАТУ ДЛЯ
PARTY
ШЕЙКЕР, ШЕЙКЕР!!!

Take Away Give Away Sofia

Design Agency: FourPlus Studio
Creative Direction and Graphic Design:
Ivaylo Nedkov
Illustration: Tsvetislava Koleva,
BorislavaWillMadeIt, Kaloyan Toshev and
Ico Ptico
Photography: Vasil Germanov

This project gathered Bulgarian artists from various fields to create a new souvenir for the city of Sofia—a postcard booklet. This postcard compilation provides tips from its authors on the alternative experiences in Sofia— bars, food, interesting sights and places to visit, extreme sports and language. Such experiences are all extremely subjective, but also quite personal.

HEIMLO: Indonesian Primates Postcard Series

Design Agency: Heimlo Studio
Illustration and Design: Annisa Aprianinda

Indonesia is located right on the earth's equator, giving it an abundance of biodiversity. One of the iconic species is the Indonesian primates, considered vulnerable due to the deforestation that often happens in Indonesia. With this series, Heimlo Studio wants to remind people of what nature has kindly given to them in the hope that more people preserve it.

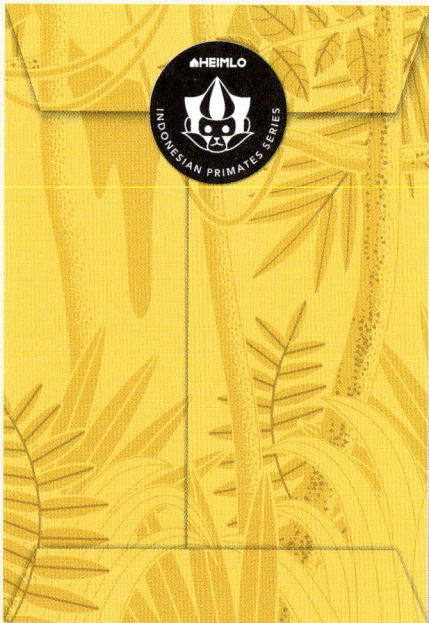

Orangutan Sumatra (Pongo abelii)

Lutung Budeng *(Trachypithecus auratus)*

Beruk *(Macaca nemestrina)*

Bekantan *(Nasalis larvatus)*

Monyet Kedih *(Presbytis thomasi)*

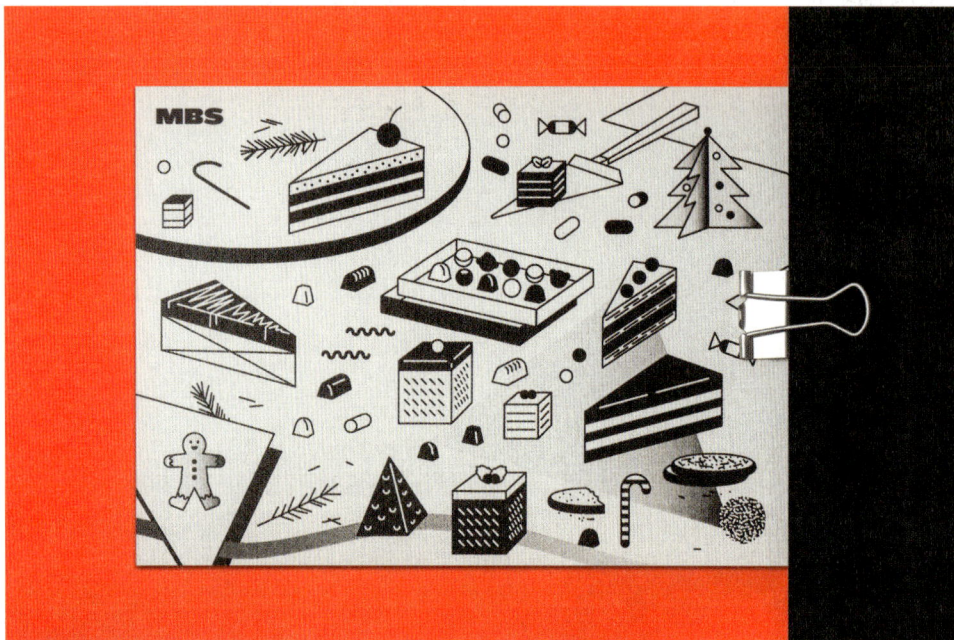

MBS Christmas Postcards

Illustration and Graphic Design:
Kata Moravszki
Client: MBS
Photography: Krisztián Lakosi

Kata Moravszki was asked to design the Christmas postcards for MBS. The whole series with two-sided printing consisted of 36 postcards. They were printed on Gmund 925 Silver Pigments and Gmund Action Electric Blood.

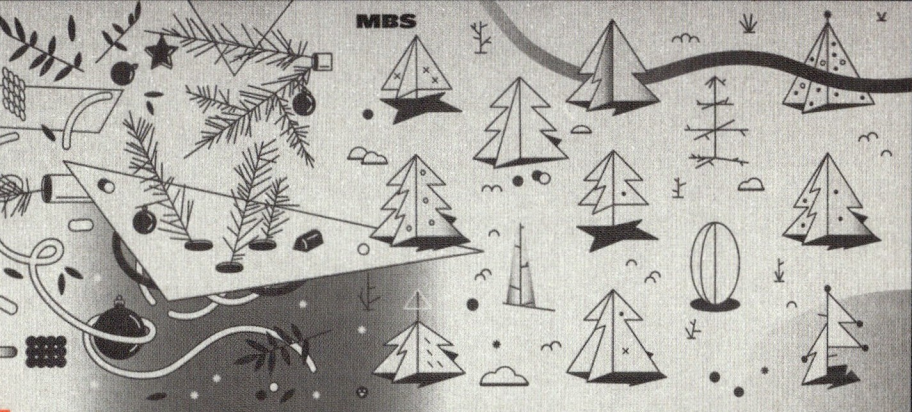

AVABAR, Seaweed Herbarium

Design Agency: Quatrième Étage
Art Direction and Design: Ophélie Raynaud and Valentin Porte
Client: Maëlle Beriou

This project is a series of prints of seaweeds, including boxes, cards, stamps and posters. Quatrième Étage aimed to refresh the concept of the traditional scientific herbarium and made it more playful and contemporary. The project contains three types of algae—AV is for green algae, AB for brown algae and AR for red algae. They were harvested in Brittany, France by Maëlle Beriou and Diego Alaguarda.

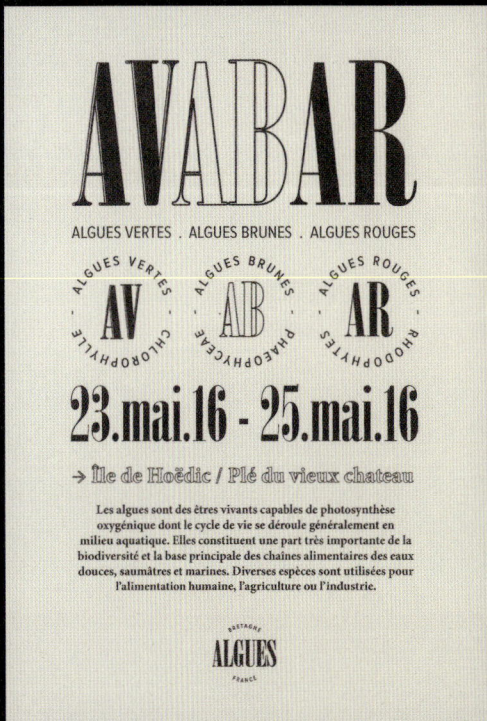

Mastocarpus stellatus
John Stackhouse
1797

—

Gigartine

Zone géographique : Manche / Atlantique / Méditerrannée

Description :

Elle est récoltée avec Chondrus crispus pour la production de carraghénanes. Le thalle est le gamétophyte. Le tétrasporophyte encroûtant était considéré comme une espèce distincte sous le nom de Petrocelis cruenta, avant qu'on ne découvre qu'il s'agissait de la même espèce.

• Île de Bréhat, Le Grand Mahou - Bretagne

Delesseria sanguinea
J.V. Lamouroux
1813

—

Algue feuille de châtaignier

Zone géographique : Manche / Atlantique / Méditerrannée

Description :

Espèce de l'infralittoral présente toute l'année mais la forme diffère selon la saison. Espèce des milieux ombragés, battus ou semi-abrités jusqu'à 30 m de profondeur. Sa présence est très abondante sous les laminaires. Cette algue rouge vif est formée d'un stipe cylindrique et de plusieurs grandes lames lancéolées (2 à 15 cm). Sur chacune d'elles apparaît une nervure centrale à partir de laquelle des veines se répartissent régulièrement et de part et d'autre. L'ensemble forme une structure pennée dont l'aspect n'est pas sans rappeler celui d'une feuille de châtaignier.

• Île de Bréhat, Le Grand Mahou - Bretagne

Rouges

Les algues rouges,
ou rhodophytes sont un
grand taxon d'algues pour
la plupart marines et
multicellulaires.
La plupart sont sessiles,
c'est-à-dire qu'elles se
développent fixées sur un
substrat quelconque.

...ées par
...entaire avec
...rophylle,
...roténoïdes
...éristiques,
...eines.
...s pendant
...térozoïque
...s d'années,
...a deuxième
...laires entre
...Orosirien il
...la faune de
...l'environ
...en puisse
...ces trois

091

Hello from Banksy
Postcards

Design: Lesha Limonov
Production: Shuba Gift Factory

This postcard series was inspired by
Banksy's self-destructed Girl with
Balloon. The key message of this postcard
series and the reference to Banksy is to
destroy the masterpiece and leave one's
own message inside the postcard. Lesha
Limonov hopes that various museums of
the world get interested in the concept of
this project.

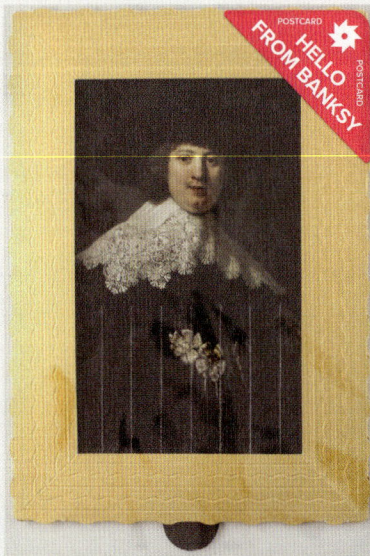

None Such Market
Postcard

Graphic Design: O.OO
Client: Envol Avec Ning

This project was designed as a branch brand for Envol Avec Ning. During the creation of the postcards and notepads for None Such Market, O.OO directly printed out the elements shown in the seasonal theme "market," such as vegetables, fruit and fish. O.OO's goal was to transform those elements from daily life and let people focus more on other kinds of "markets."

None Such Market
Postcard : Recycle paper, Soy ink
Net Wt/Ct
5.00g
Unit Price
$ 70.0/g
Total Price
$ 350.0
Packed On
Jun 03,17
04:42 PM
Sell By
mm dd yy
SAFE HANDLING INSTRUCTIONS
THIS PRODUCT WAS PREPARED FROM INSPECTED AND PASSED MEAT AND/OR POULTRY. SOME FOOD PROUCTS MAY CONTAIN BACTERIA THAT COULD CAUSE ILLNESS IF THAT PRODUCT IS MISHANDLED OR COOKED IMPROPERLY. FOR YOUR PROTECTION, FOLLOW THESE SAFE HANDLING INSTRUCTIONS. KEEP REFRIGERATED OR FROZEN. THAW IN REFRIGERATOR OR MICROWAVE. KEEP RAW MEAT AND POULTRY SEPARATE FROM OTHER FOODS.
EAN

New Year Greeting Cards

Design Agency: CICATA, Inc.
Art Direction: Koichiro Kitamoto
Design: Koichiro Kitamoto and Sheila Gamba
Photography: Shogo Takebayashi

In Japan, there is a tradition of sending New Year's greeting cards, called nengajo. Every year, CICATA tackles its design with special printing techniques such as foiling, silk screen printing, embossing, letterpress printing and so on to make these cards memorable.

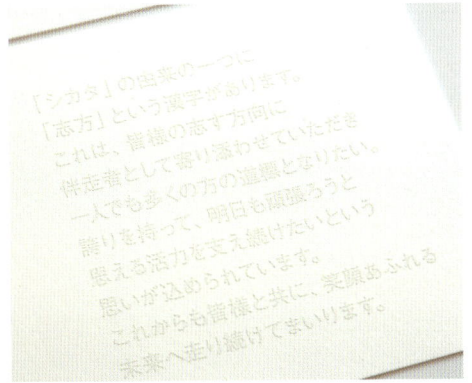

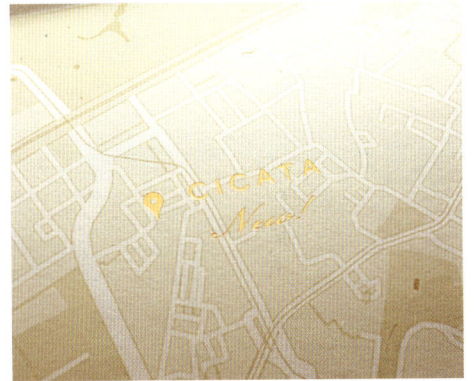

2019 Golden Pig
Chinese New Year Card

Art Direction and Design: Chen Hao-En
Photography: Ferguson Chang

The pig is the main theme of this design.
Chen Hao-En used the yellow color to
complement the overall design. Yellow is
not only an outstanding shade, but also
an auspicious symbol with an abundance
of good meanings and omens. Yellow
also symbolizes earth. The combination
of yellow, blue and silver makes the pig
appear in 3D. The design was further
enhanced with hot stamping technology.
And the finishing touches are put together
nicely with embossing on quality yellow-
based paper.

A por la Rentrée

Design Agency: Sr. y Sra. Wilson
Printing: Lentejas Press

This card is used to celebrate the rentrée (return) after the summer holidays. This card was sent to other designers and studios in Barcelona to encourage them to get them back to work with energy and happiness. This A5-sized card used a risograph technique, and was printed in yellow and blue. The overlap of two colors creates a unique third color.

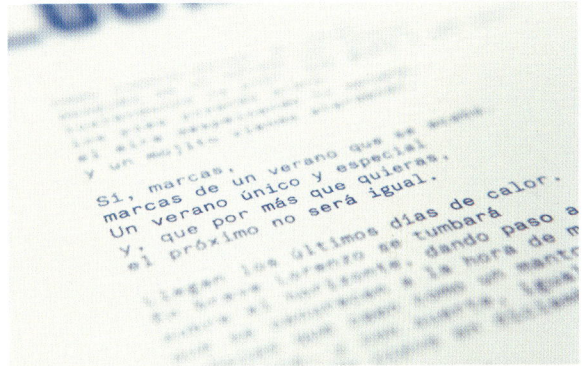

4th Anniversary Greeting Card of Backer-Founder

Design: Yu-Qian Huang
Client: Backer-Founder
Photography: Zhi-Yang Zeng

Backer-Founder is a leading crowd-funding consultancy in Asia and regards itself as a courageous ship guiding the way. For the fourth anniversary of Backer-Founder, Yu-Qian Huang designed a greeting card. The main visual is an admiralty chart—every client can feel like a crew member who looks back on the adventures and feels proud of the achievement.

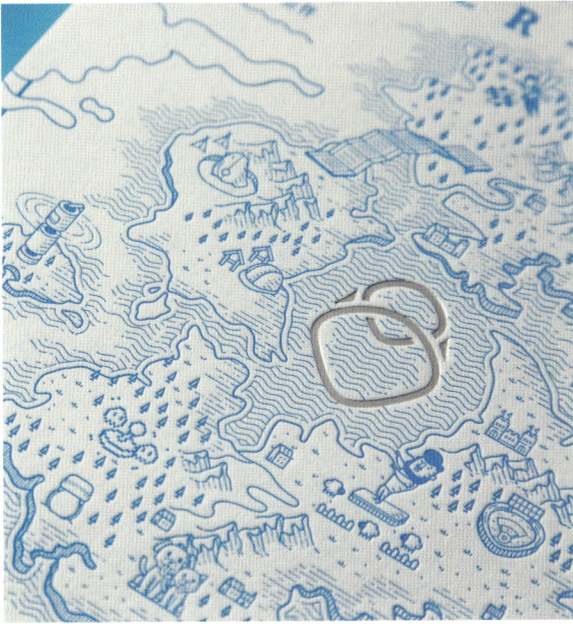

4th Anniversary

BACKER-FOUNDER

親愛的貝殼夥伴

貝殼放大在今年 10 月 20 日就滿 4 歲生日了，這一路上，我們與超過 200 個團隊齊力推動集資案件，也不時在各個社會議題中發聲。截至 9 月底，貝殼放大累積的案件參與人次已達 40 萬人，累積總集資金額超過 9 億元！

貝殼放大在「Backer」與「Founder」之間，勤奮地恪守著中間連結線的角色，期待更多有如星星般的夢想，都因我們的牽線而閃閃發光。而過去這一年，貝殼放大積極地嘗試不同領域的拓展，包含大型企業品牌形象的規劃與執行，也累積了許多美好的故事和經驗。

「群眾集資」是一條把夢想放大的航道！值得的事，都不容易，我們也未首選過好走的路。「夥伴」是我們最珍貴的寶藏，這一路上謝謝您的支持與指導，未來或許偶過暗礁埋伏、會有大浪顛顛，但新的年度，請與我們一起不放棄航行！

貝殼放大 執行長　林大涵

2019 Red Envelope Set

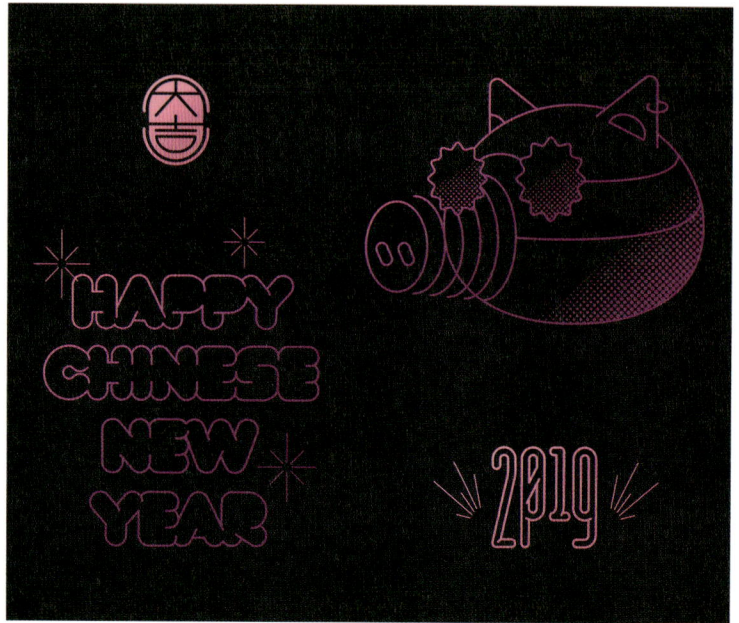

Design Agency: EARLYBIRDS DESIGN
Creative Direction: Arron Chang

The main visual of this project is the pig and the Chinese character "da ji." EARLYBIRDS DESIGN aimed to avoid the cliché by using the geometrical lines and dot printing to represent a modern, retro style. For the red envelope, EARLYBIRDS DESIGN selected Japanese Tant Paper in carmine and dark purple and achieved a better texture by fog foil stamping.

Season's Greetings

Design Agency: Thinking Room
Creative Direction: Eric Widjaja
Design: Evan Wijaya

Every year, Thinking Room gives each
of its clients a Christmas basket with a
Christmas card attached. In 2017, the
card design evoked the classic feeling
of traditional Christmas cards. The
cards were personalized by putting the
clients' names on the "nice list," which
is traditionally used by Santa Claus,
along with the names of famous graphic
designers. The colors were picked from
vintage Christmas cards to invoke the
classic vibe of traditional Christmas
cards. Green and red were chosen, too,
but were made less vibrant.

Year of the Dog
Greeting Card

Art Direction and Design: Canwei Lai

This project is based on the theme—"all lucky things come in 2018." Inspired by the linking game *Lianliankan*, which is popular in China, the designer displays the dog's different expressions blended into the patterns "2018."

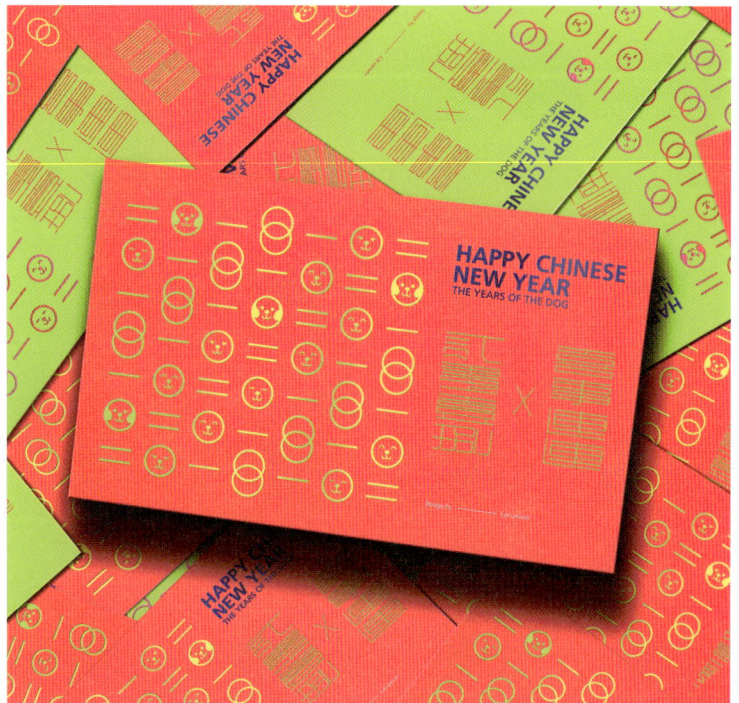

2019 Chinese New Year Card—Everything is Good

Art Direction and Design: Lin Wei-Cheng
Photography: Ferguson Chang

Chinese New Year is a traditional yearly cultural celebration. The year 2019 was symbolized by the pig from the Chinese zodiac. Lin Wei-Cheng used geometric shapes to display the pigs on the card. The orange and red colors represent the happiness and prosperity of the new year. In addition, the gold and silver stamping and embossing adds texture.

Greeting Card and Red Envelope of TRA

Design: Ciou Bo Hao
Copywriting: Hu Bi Zong

The key visual for this project was the combination of trains and pigs. The "locomotive pig" pulls the carriages with traditional Chinese new year elements, such as spring couplets, lanterns and firecrackers. Meanwhile, the different assemblies of carriages form the typeface "2019" and show the unique Chinese new year's atmosphere of TRA.

Letter Press
Christmas Card

Design: Seolhee Yang

This series of cards celebrate Christmas with the slogan "Happy Merry." Christmas symbols like a snowman, Rudolph and other reindeer are on the center of the cards. Seolhee Yang also decided the cards should look like ornaments and used geometric shapes.

Christmas Postcards

Illustration and Design: Kinga Offert

Inspired by the tradition of caroling still present in some regions in Poland, Kinga Offert designed this set of four postcards. Kinga said the essence of caroling is the exchange of gifts. The carolers dress in funny costumes and visit farms, bringing wishes of harvest, health and good luck. In return, they receive Christmas treats or small donations. The omission of a household is sometimes regarded as a bad sign.

Los Tipo-Totems

Design: Mattia Zingale
Photography: Mattia Zingale

After taking part in the yearly #36daysoftype, Mattia Zingale decided to transform the 36 typefaces from digital to print. As a collection of 36 postcards, this project features a typographic totem designed by Mattia, taking inspiration from the totemic figures all over the world. Mattia chose 200 g/m² Favini uncoated paper and five different colors to meet the need for function and aesthetics. The box for the postcards was made with a recycled 300 g/m² paper. To avoid single-use plastic in the packaging, Mattia used an adhesive Velcro fastener, which allows for continuous usage with no material waste.

New Year's Card

Illustration and Graphic Design:
Studio-Takeuma

This series is for celebrating the new year. Each animal in this series belongs to the 12 Japanese zodiac signs, which originated from the Chinese zodiac.

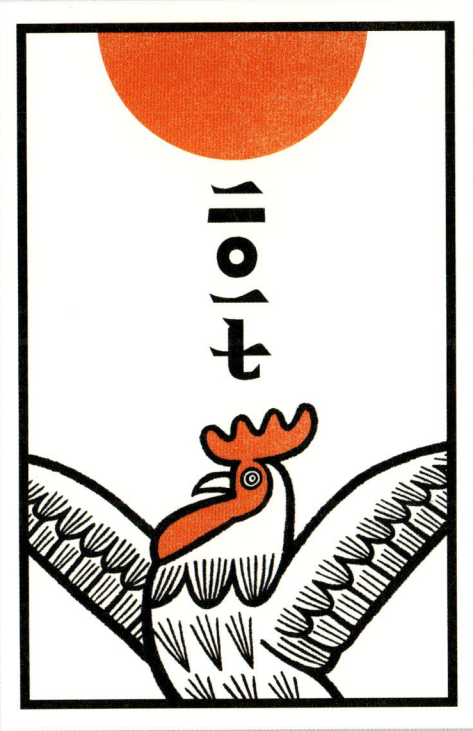

2019 Chinese New Year Greeting Card

Design Agency: TSUBAKI STUDIO
Printing: Imprint Kepong

In this design, TUSBAKI broke away from the norm by embracing the cool colors of green, purple, and turquoise instead of the traditional red. This design embraces the shift in perception of the modern-day Chinese new year. For instance, cherished moments of the festival are depicted in modern illustrations featuring the iconic lion dance, fireworks and many other elements of Chinese new year. Printed on 350gsm chipboard, this card is coated in Pantone colors of turquoise and violet, topped off with rose gold hot stamping.

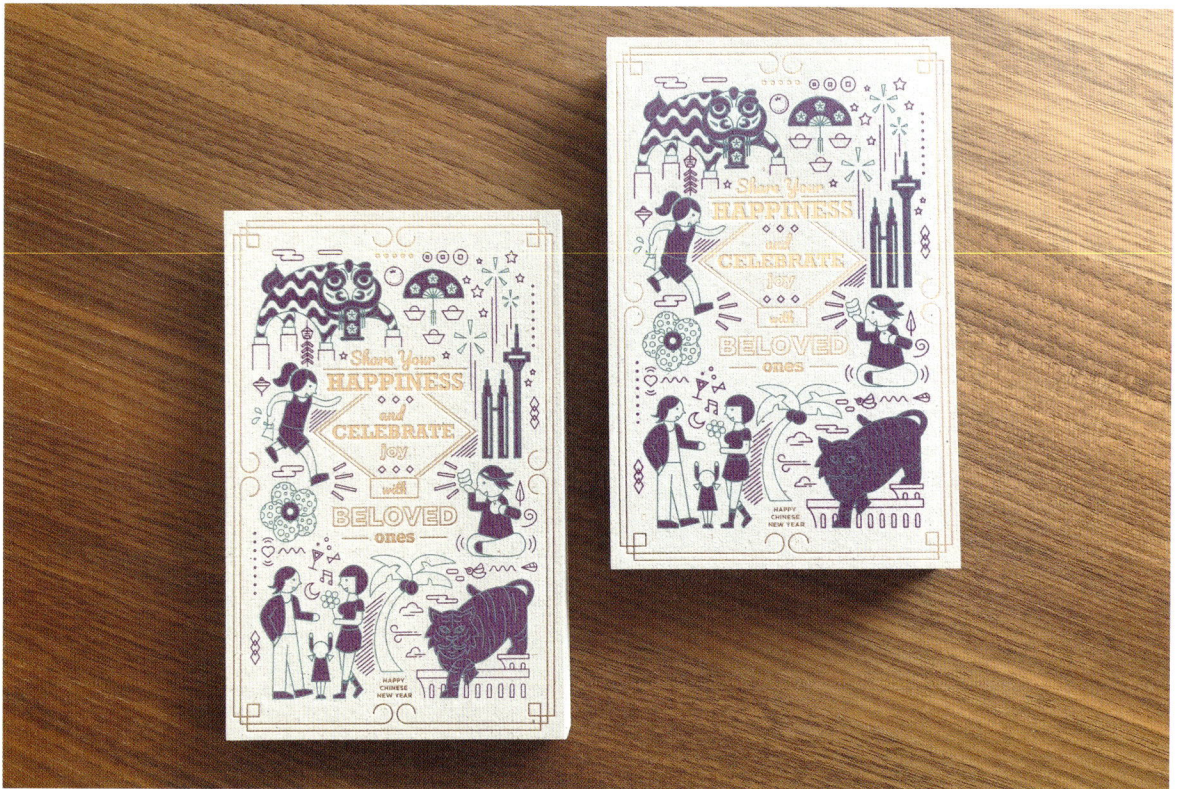

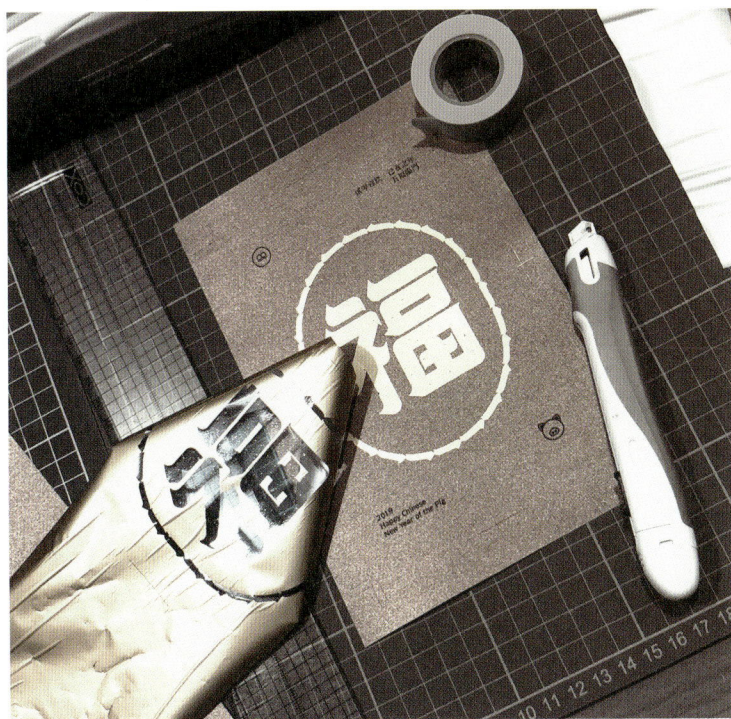

Chinese New Year Cards 2019

Design: Axter Chu Chon Kit

The theme of this series is fo (fortune), lu (emolument), shou (longevity) and hei (happiness). In the traditional Chinese new year, these four words have significant meaning. In terms of the production process, Axter Chu Chon Kit began his typography work on the computer and printed it using a laser printer. The four words, fo, lu, shou and hei, were tooled in gold by hand.

2019.5 Cat Year Card

Design: Cecil Tang
Photography: Cecil Tang

In Chinese mythology, the cat is not part of the Chinese zodiac because of the trick of the rat. As half of 2019 or the year of the pig had passed, Cecil Tang decided to make a card for the cat before 2020 or the year of the rat began. Like a hidden Easter egg, this year card displays a unique graphic composition.

STAMPS

Postage stamp design has had a long history since a profile bust of Queen Victoria was adopted in 1840 for the Penny Black, the world's first adhesive stamp. Because a stamp is small, its graphic design plays an important role. There are four major categories for the graphics of a stamp design: portrait bust, emblem, number and picture. Nowadays, artists, designers and administrative officials choose the subject matter and the method of printing stamps. Meanwhile, digital stamps have become more and more popular.

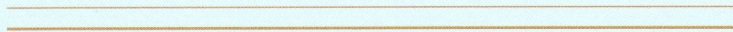

Queen Elizabeth II
65th Anniversary of the Coronation

Design Agency: Paprika
Client: Canada Post
Image Source: Princess Elizabeth (1951) /
Yousuf Karsh, © Estate of Yousuf Karsh

June 2, 2018 marked the 65th anniversary
of the coronation of Queen Elizabeth
II. Paprika designed a series of new
stamps utilizing the famous portrait done
in July 1951 by Armenian-Canadian
photographer Yousuf Karsh, which is
well-known to generations of Canadians.

Bruch

Art Direction and Creative Direction:
Bruch—Idee & Form
Letterpress: Infinitive Factory

The branding for Bruch is a reference to
the name and the tagline "Idee & Form."
Defined shapes, color and typography
were arranged according to an idea and
the name "Bruch" was communicated in
a subtle way. The vivid and changeable
arrangements are also a reference to
the studio's projects—as each aims to
be individual. One of the most important
touchpoints for this new design was
postage stamps. Bruch wanted to have
an immediate eye-catcher on the
envelope to stand out. The various stamps
communicate the studio's approach and
ability to create an impact.

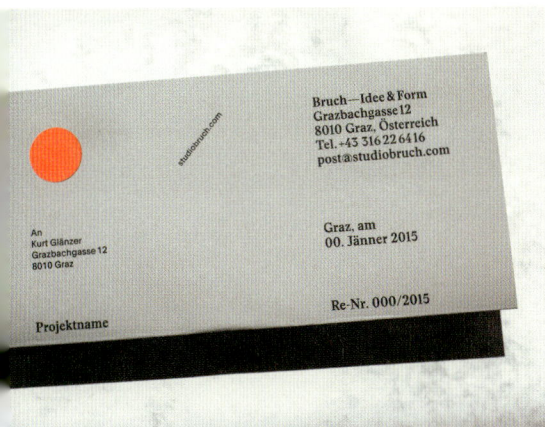

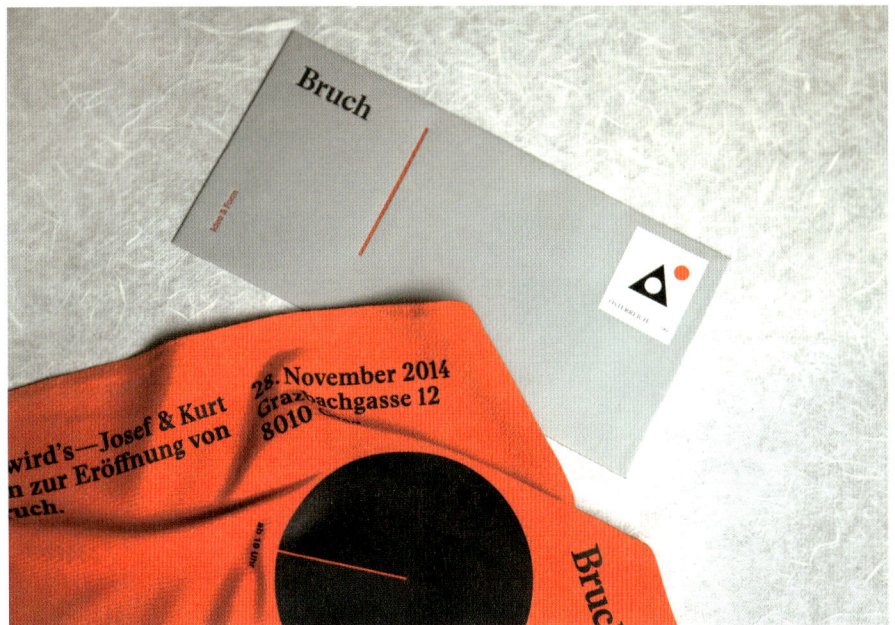

Commemorative Karl Marx Stamp

Design: Thomas Mayfried
Issuer: German Federal Ministry of the Finance
Image Source: John Mayall (1875) / courtesy of the
International Institute of Social History, Amsterdam

In 2018, on the occasion of Karl Marx's 200th birthday, the German Federal Ministry of Finance launched a commemorative stamp. Thomas Mayfried reworked a portrait of Karl Marx, which was taken by the London photographer John Mayall in 1875. This picture shows Marx, as described by his colleague Friedrich Engels, "completely in his cheerful, victorious Olympian peace." Engels chose this photograph to distribute among his comrades as a carte-de-visite in a print run of 1,000 and the image became iconic. Through a thick grid of black and white lines, Thomas abstracts what is probably the most frequently reproduced portrait of Marx.

Age of Empires: The Conquerors

Illustration and Design: Roy Vu

The Age of Empires: The Conquerors was inspired by the game of the same name from a long time ago when Roy Vu was a child. With his love of this game and history, Roy came up with the idea of drawing in the style of personal visualization, thereby conveying the soul of each character in different periods of history with the recurring beautiful memories.

Destination Greece

Design: Mike Karolos

This stamp collection is a self-initiated project that aims to show the beautiful side of Greece in an illustrative, abstract style. Greece has been a trending topic in the past few years due to the economic and refugee crisis. So, with the current social and political upheaval, people sometimes forget that Greece is one of the most beautiful and safest places on earth. It combines nature and history, amazing beaches and mesmerizing food. In this collection, Mike Karolos tried to use his own style to show some very characteristic places and scenes in Greece, such as Greek islands, ancient artifacts, landmarks, beaches, traditional houses and food.

TBSC

Design: Cris Ruiz

TBSC is a personal project inspired by the state of Tabasco, located in southern Mexico, a place with great natural, cultural and gastronomic richness. With the use of Adobe Illustrator, Cris Ruiz showed cheerful, warm and friendly characteristics through this project. And the viewers can feel the vibe of the people of Tabasco.

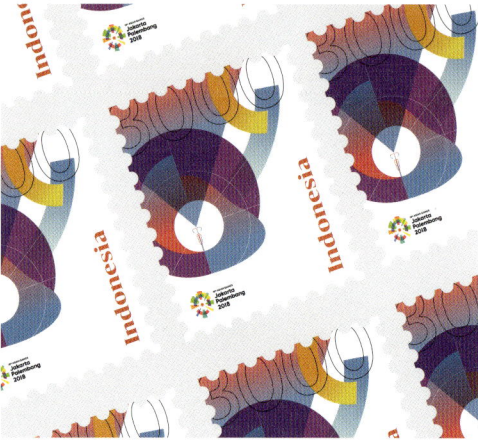

Experimental Postage Stamp Design Asian Games 2018

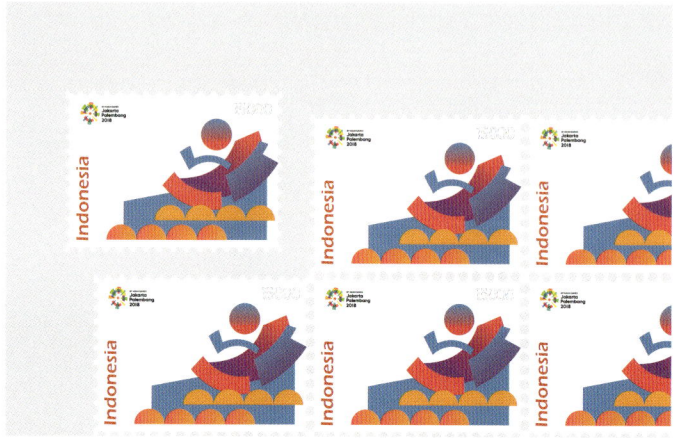

Design: Rosi Indra Satria
Image Source: Official Logo of Asian Games 2018

Asian Games is one of the biggest sporting events in Asia. Stamps are one of the proper media to welcome the sports event. Rosi Indra Satria tried to make a more attractive design. Inspired by characteristics of several sports and vintage Swiss stamps, Rosi took combined them with some elements of the official logo to represent modern, avant-garde, attraction, vitality and timelessness in accordance with the spirit of the Asian Games and the millennials.

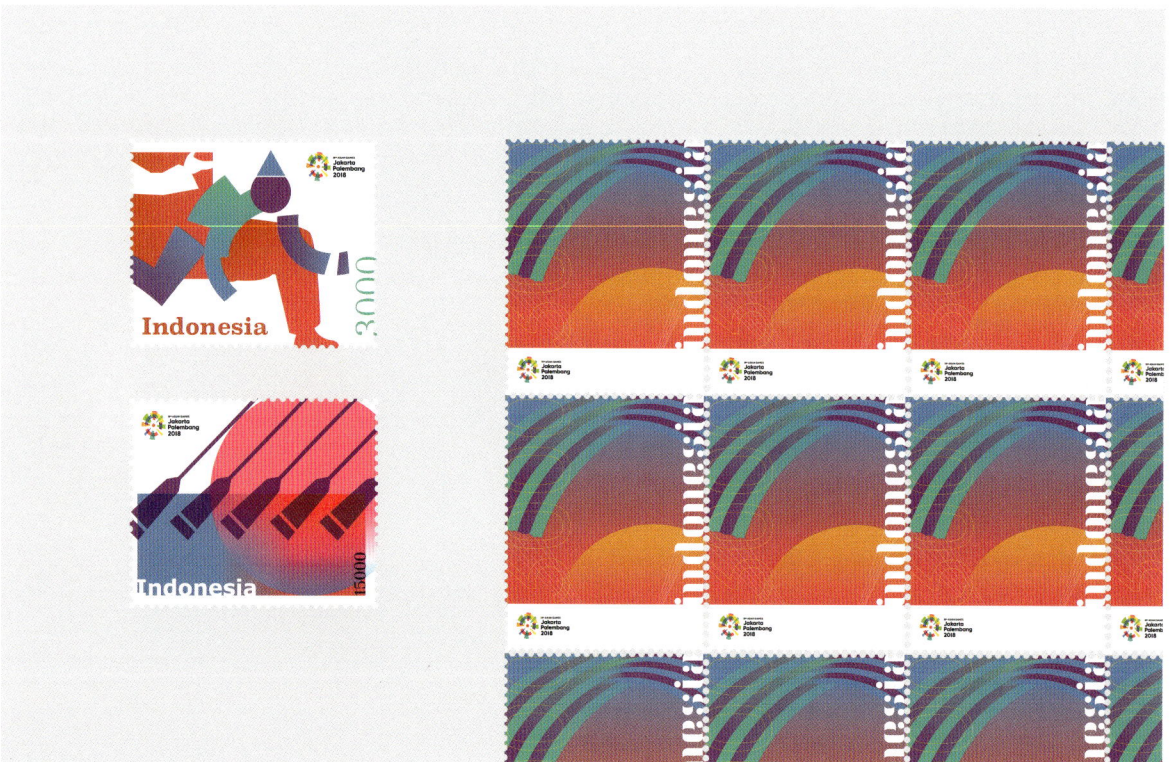

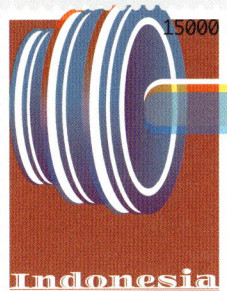

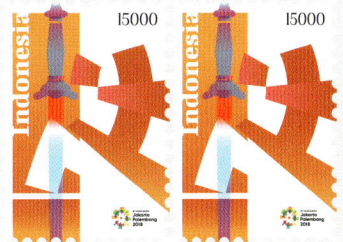

AFRICAN ELEPHANT	Loxodonta africana	CHEETAH	Acinonyx jubatus	PLAINS ZEBRA	Equus quagga
ZAMBIA ZMK 2.50		ZAMBIA ZMK 2.50		ZAMBIA ZMK 2.50	

WHITE RHINOCEROS · Ceratotherium simum · BOTSWANA BWP 2.70
HIPPOPOTAMUS · Hippopotamus amphibius · BOTSWANA BWP 2.70
GIRAFFE · Giraffa camelopardalis · BOTSWANA BWP 2.70

BABOON · Papio · SOUTH AFRICA ZAR 10
IMPALA · Aepyceros melampus · ZIMBABWE ZWR 65
AFRICAN WILD DOG · Lycaon pictus · ZAMBIA ZMK 2.50

WILDEBEEST · Connochaetes taurinus · ZIMBABWE ZWR 65
AFRICAN LION · Panthera leo · BOTSWANA BWP 2.70
SERVAL · Felis serval · ZAMBIA ZMK 2.50

African Animal Stamps

Design: Gökçe Yiğit

When Gökçe Yiğit found a stamp on a street in Africa, it inspired her to design a series of timeless stamps for African wild animals, such as the cheetah, baboon and serval. As Gökçe Yiğit's poetry says, animals rule time, unlike human beings.

SERVAL · Felis serval · ZAMBIA ZMK 2.50

FIRST DAY OF ISSUE
BOTSWANA
AFRICAN STAMP
2 AUGUST 1993

AFRICAN LION · Panthera leo · BOTSWANA BWP 2.70

MUTI's Stamp Collection

Illustration: MUTI

Both Jolly Holly and Roma are stamps referring to the celebration of Christmas and the tale of Romulus and Remus. MUTI illustrated a set of icons for Everyday Stamps, a private photo journal app that lets users collect their own thoughts and mark the moments in everyday life. Each stamp represents a mood, which the users then add to their photos.

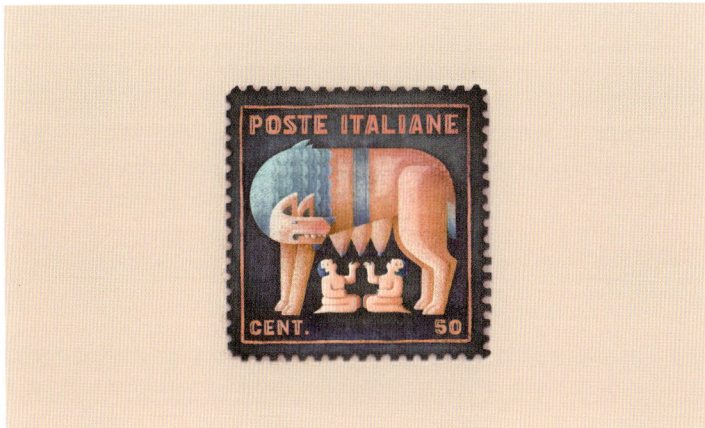

Socovos Magazine

For the year 2017, the editorial concept of *Socovos Magazine* was "a magazine and a stamp to share the town of Socovos, Spain with outsiders." This concept led Rubio y del Amo to present for its cover, a folding postcard design, like a retro souvenir. The colorful illustrations on those postcards are symbolic places in Socovos, which are regarded as the collective memory of the local people. What's more, a serial of customized stamps and an invitation on the first page of the magazine are attached.

Design Agency: Rubio y del Amo
Illustration: Guillermo Rubio and Dario Ferrante
Design: Guillermo Rubio

Digamos al resto del mundo lo especial que es nuestro pueblo y nuestras fiestas. Por eso, este año la revista te invita a mandar una postal a todo aquel que aún no conoce Socovos ni su Feria. Te invita a compartir la suerte que tenemos de ser socoveños.

La Comisión de Fiestas

Maison Tangible

Design: Jérôme Masi
Client: Maison Tangible

Jérôme Masi was commissioned by
Maison Tangible to illustrate three stamps
and to answer "L'interview Timbrée."
The stamp was once a link between
people, cultures and territories, but it's
changed dramatically as technology
evolved. This stamp series reflects the
theme of universality and the effacement
of borders, illustrating a great melting pot
of people.

Hello Stamp Design

Design: Muhammed Sajid

Muhammed Sajid designed the stamps called Hello to commemorate the telephone's evolution. The viewers can clearly see the earliest inventions and high-tech communication equipment at the same time.

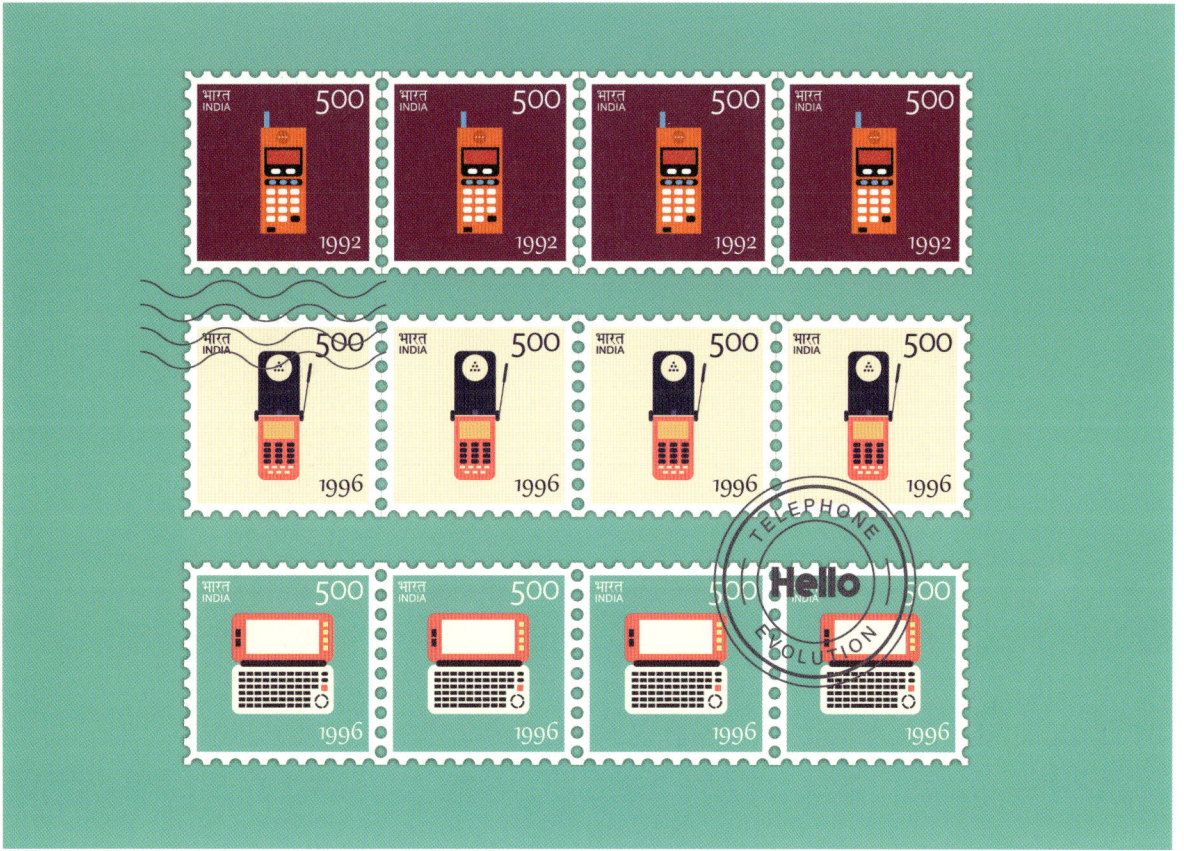

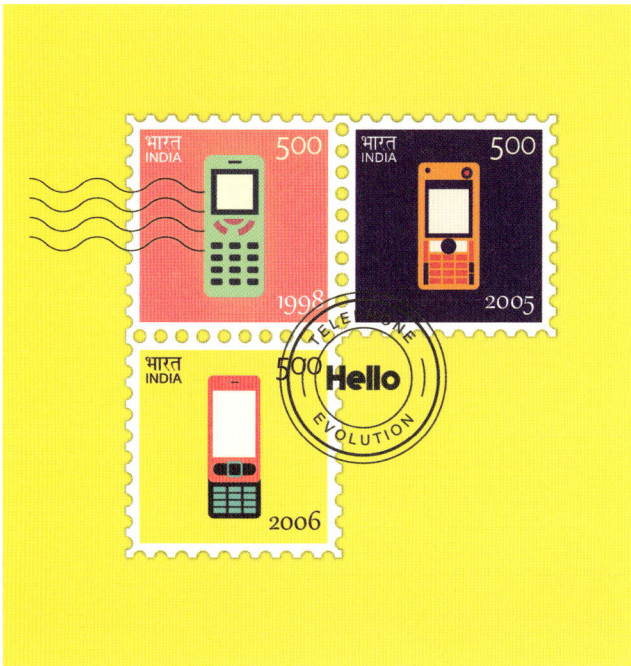

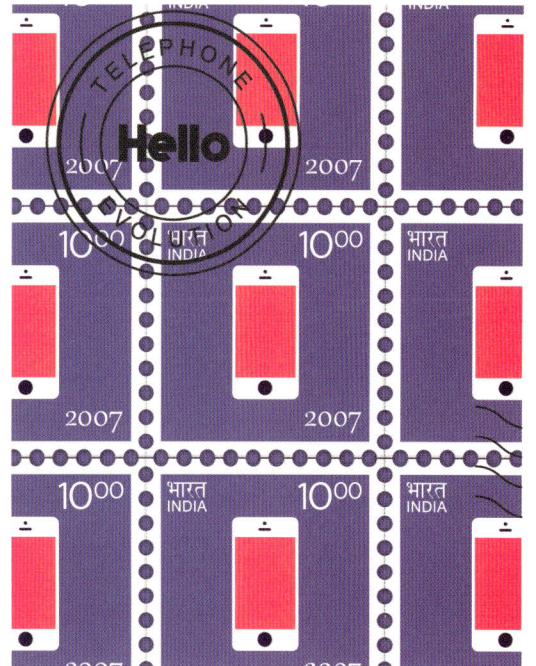

Charles De Gaulle
Memorial Stamps

Design Agency: Atelier1234567890
Design: Nicolas Thioulouse and Marion Begue
Client: Memorial Charles De Gaulle and
La Poste

On June 18, 1940, Charles De Gaulle made a speech on BBC calling for all French people to resist the invasion of the Nazis. These commemorative stamps commemorate the 75th anniversary of that speech. The graphics are based on the power of words and the intonation of speech. Blankness, breathing and screaming are transcribed through lines and colors. Meanwhile, the dark background reveals the shadow of war.

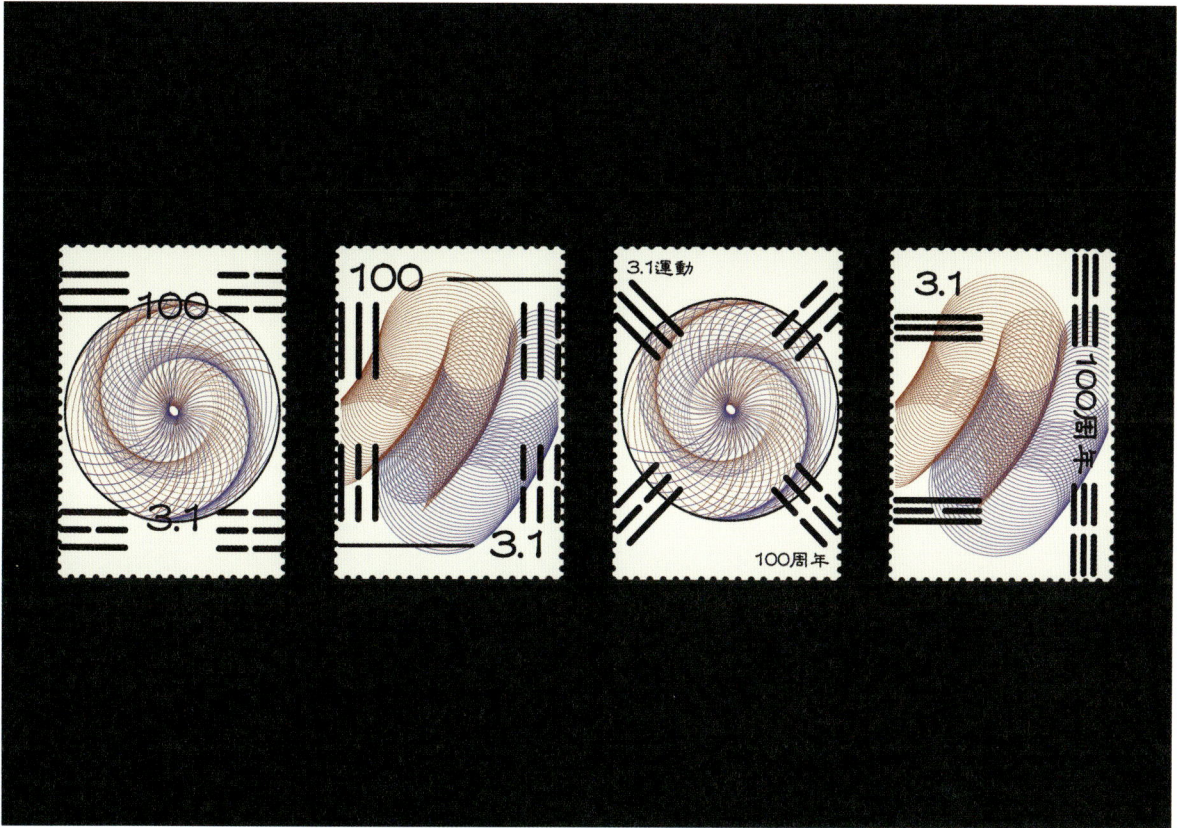

The Korean 3.1 Independence Movement

Design: Sesol Choi

This stamp design celebrating the centennial of the March 1st Movement of 1919. They represent Taegukgi (the Korean nation flag) with a red and blue geometric pattern constantly moving in one direction. Also, the four trigrams referring to heaven, earth, water and fire are an important visual. And Taegukgi's white background symbolizes purity and peacefulness.

Formula 1

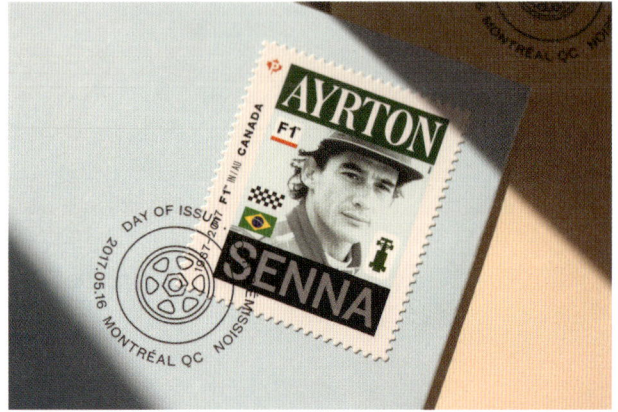

Design Agency: Paprika
Client: Canada Post
Image Source: Sir Jackie Stewart (Sutton-Images.com), Gilles Villeneuve (ullstein bild / Getty Images), Ayrton Senna (Rainer W. Schlegelmilch / Getty Images, © of ASE under license from Instituto Ayrton Senna), Michael Schumacher (Michael Cooper / Getty Images Sport Classic) and Lewis Hamilton (Jonathan Cottam / Contour / Getty Images)

In celebration of the 50th anniversary of Formula 1 racing in Canada, Canada Post issued a supercharged set of stamps featuring five of the fastest drivers ever to capture the checkered flag at the Formula 1 Grand Prix du Canada–each representing a different decade in the history of the race.

Retro Modern Stamp Concepts

Design: Mohammad Rasoulipour

Inspired by an online project called Basic Stamps, Duane Dalton Mohammad Rasoulipour reused some of his old designs from a soccer shirt project to create retro, but modern stamp concepts.

State Stamps 2019

Design: Ethan Fender

Ethan Fender launched his project, State Stamps, in 2016 during the presidential election in America. Witnessing a lot of divisions among political parties, Ethan wanted to show the beauty of each state in a simple and iconic way. There are alternative versions of each stamp and these are the most revised ones and scaled down to size.

The Fête des Vignerons 2019 Stamps

Design Agency: Balmer Hählen
Client: Swiss Post

Balmer Hählen made three special stamps in collaboration with Swiss Post. The design of stamps was based on the official poster of the Fête des Vignerons 2019, which was also created by Balmer Hählen. The stamps are a variant of that poster in which the three motifs, a bunch of grapes, the sun and a starling, depict the life cycle of the vine. Fête des Vignerons is a unique winegrowers' festival held in Vevey, Switzerland.

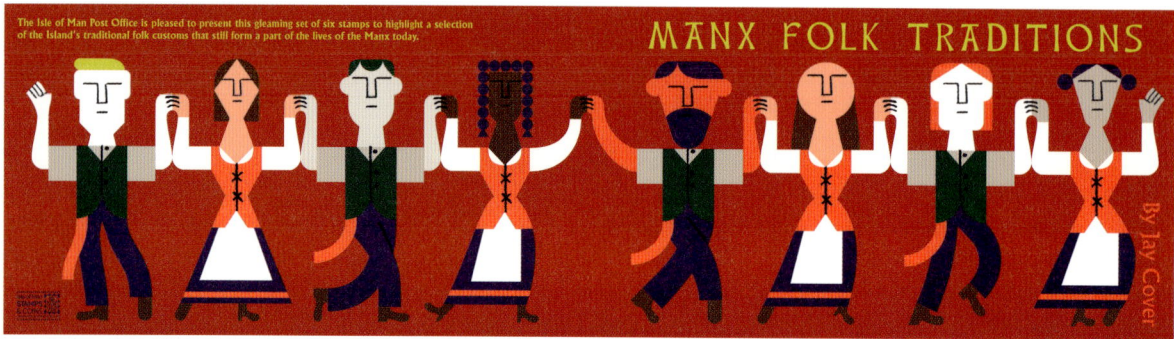

The Isle of Man Post Office is pleased to present this gleaming set of six stamps to highlight a selection of the Island's traditional folk customs that still form a part of the lives of the Manx today.

MANX FOLK TRADITIONS

By Jay Cover

Manx Folk Traditions

Design: Jay Cover
Client: Isle of Man Post Office

Manx Folk Traditions is a set of stamps commissioned by the Isle of Man post office, which celebrates the Isle of Man's winter and autumn folk traditions. Jay Cover took a very graphic approach to the stamps, taking inspiration from Celtic and Norse wooden and stone carvings, drawing reference to the origin of most of the traditions featured in the stamps.

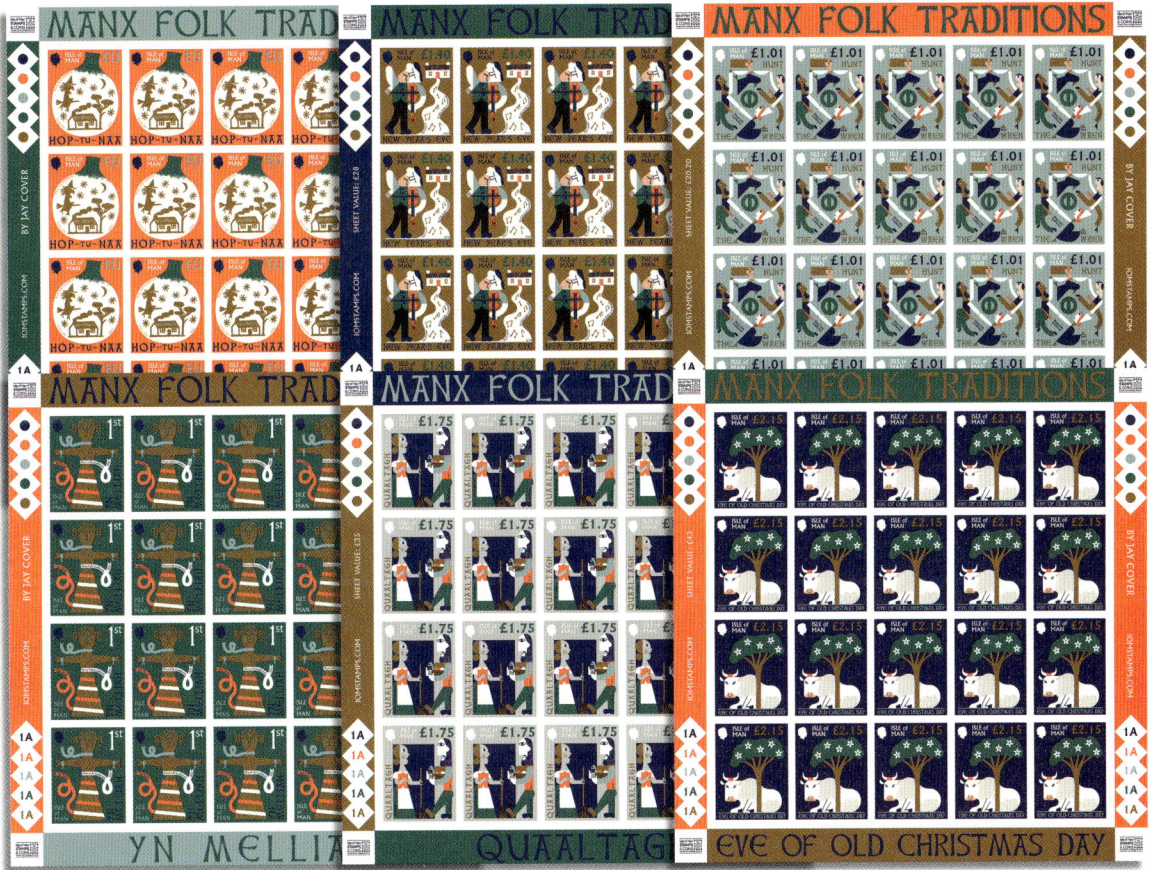

Illustrator, artist and educator Jay Cover was born and raised on the Isle of Man. He studied Foundation Art & Design at the Isle of Man College under Ian Coulson before moving to Yorkshire to study BA Visual Communication at Leeds College of Art in 2004. He now lives and works in Hastings, after spending some time honing and developing his craft in London.

Alongside his art practice, Jay teaches illustration at Camberwell College of Arts and is one third of artist collective Nous Vous, who have been collaborating on large scale visual art projects for over ten years. Producing animations for Facebook and Cheerios, beer labels for Camden Town Brewery, books for Princeton Architectural Press and Tate Publishing, advertising campaigns for The Southbank Centre and Greenman Festival, alongside numerous other projects.

In this set of stamps Jay has adopted the bold, geometric shapes and visual economy of Celtic and Norse wood carving, using a colour palette derived from Manx tartan. These stamp designs aim to breath fresh life into our folk traditions.

Year of the Rooster

Design Agency: Paprika
Client: Canada Post

This series consists of stamps with domestic and international rates, showcasing the striking designs by Paprika. The golden lines on the international stamps reflect the rooster's stately profile, while the undulating pattern on the domestic stamps features the fowl in a full image with its chest puffed out with pride.

HKBU COMM 50th Anniversary Visual Design

Design Agency: Milkxhake
Illustration: Saki Ho
Design: Javin Mo, Saki Ho
Client: School of Communication, Hong Kong Baptist University (China)

Saki Ho created a visual identity for the 50th anniversary of School of Communication at Hong Kong Baptist University in 2018. The identity began with the commemorative stamp's design as they are classic, iconic communication tools, as well as tiny canvases for visual messages. The four sets of stamps have distinctive colors and illustrations, corresponding to three study streams – Academy of Film, Communication Studies and Journalism. The last set represents the School of Communication, in general.

Swiss Type Designers
Stamp Collection

Design: Gwen Yixin Zhang

This is a commemorative stamp collection of Swiss-type designers' typography designs. This collection included Max Miedinger's Helvetica, Adrain Frutiger's Avenir, Karl Gerstner's Gerstner, Marco Ganz's Veto, Bruno Maag's Royalty and Dominique Kerber's Cast. Inspired by the geometric shapes of these typefaces, Gwen Yixin Zhang took one or two elements from each font and played with their characteristics to form the stamps' graphs.

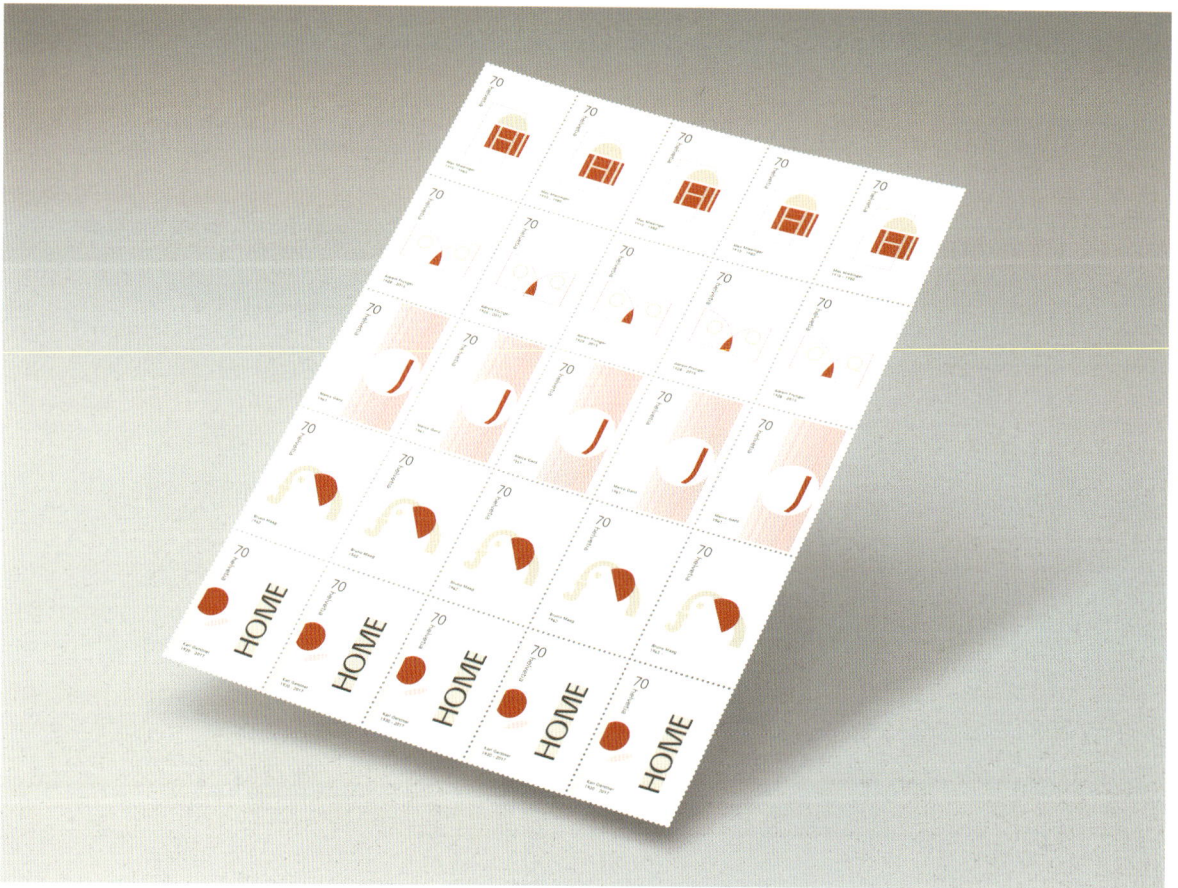

70 helvetia — Bruno Maag 1962 -

70 helvetia — Dominique Kerber 1980 -

70 helvetia — Marco Ganz 1961 -

70 helvetia — Max Miedinger 1910 - 1980

70 helvetia — Max Miedinger 1910 - 1980

70 helvetia — Max Miedinger 1910 - 1980

70 helvetia — Karl Gerstner 1930 - 2017 — HOME

70 helvetia — Karl Gerstner 1930 - 2017 — HOME

70 helvetia — Karl Gerstner 1930 - 2017 — HOME

70 helvetia — Adrain Frutiger 1928 - 2015

70 helvetia — Adrain Frutiger 1928 - 2015

70 helvetia — Adrain Frutiger 1928 - 2015

Xing Shi Shan

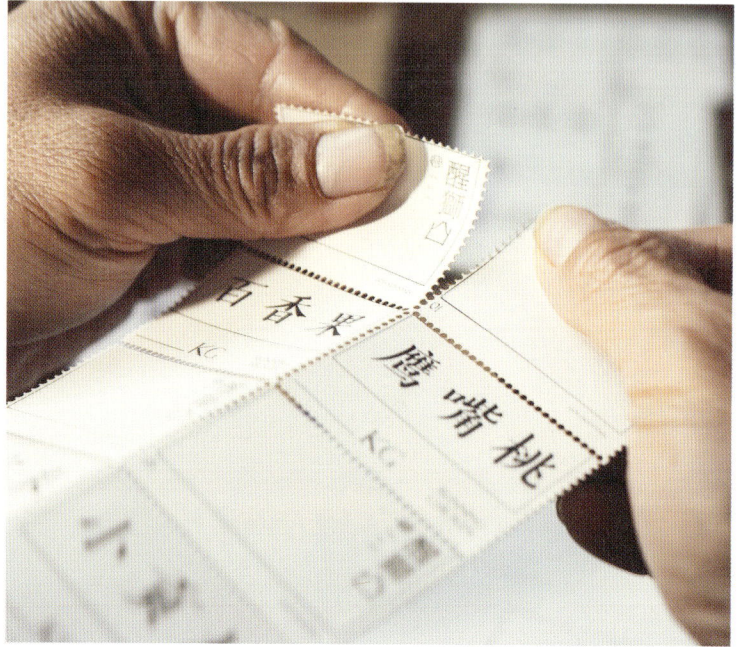

Design Agency: One More
Art Direction: Huang Fupeng
Creative Direction: Xia Jiangnan
Design Direction: Mao Jian
Illustration: Gong Chaoping
Design: Huang Junjie

Xing Shi Shan (Xing Shi Mountain) is a project to help poor people living in mountainous areas sell their products in the market. One More thought out the most suitable visual for this project, a stamp that used a symbol connecting the mountainous area with the urban city.

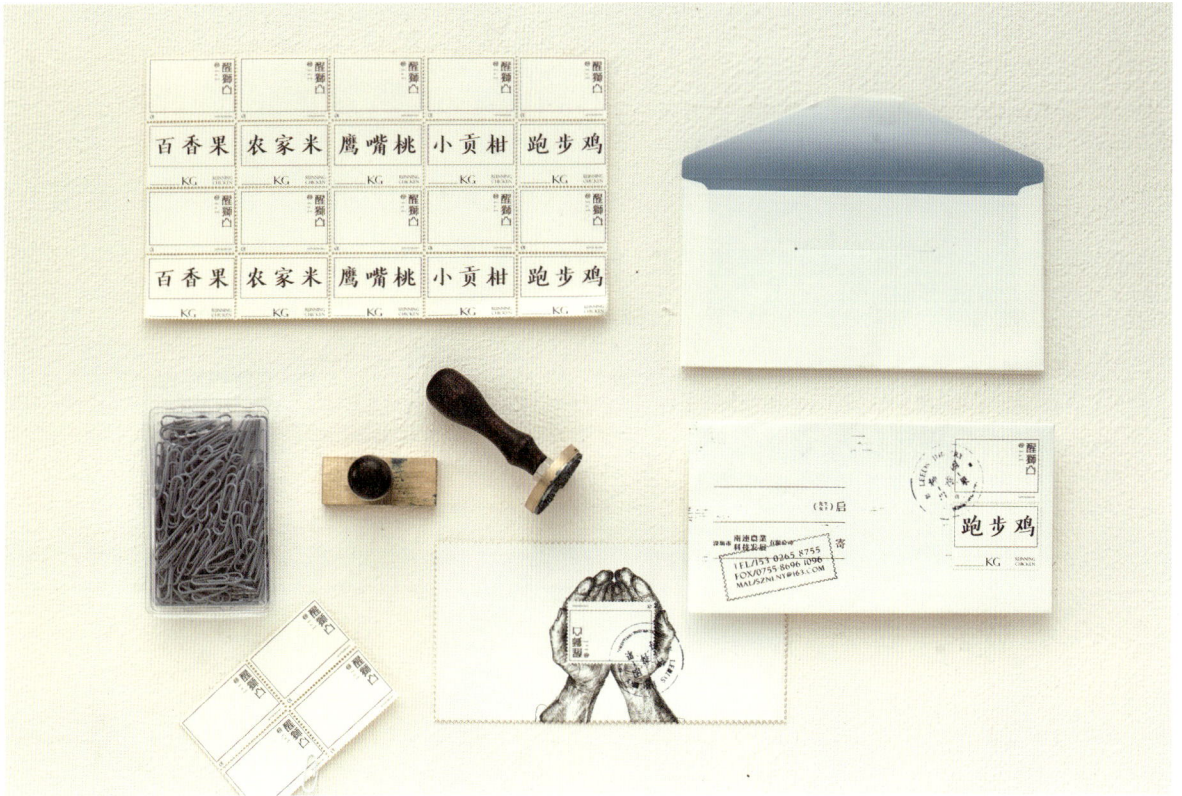

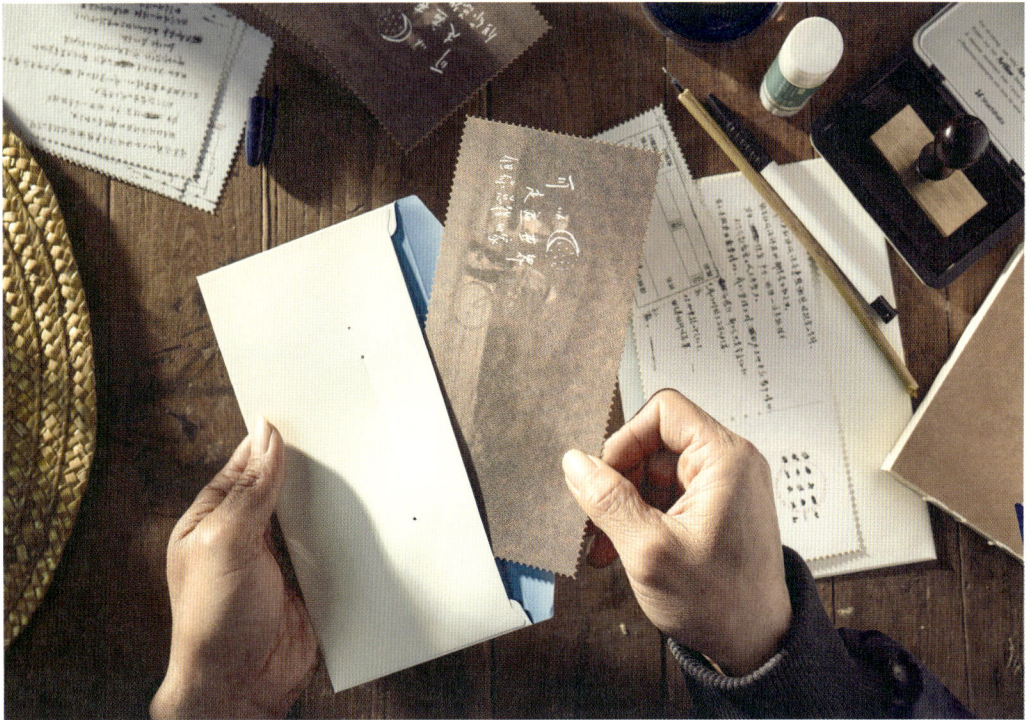

36 Days of Type 2017
Stamp Collection

Design: Meroo Seth

This is Meroo Seth's contribution to the fourth edition of the 36 Days of Type Challenge 2017. She created a stamp collection for each letter.

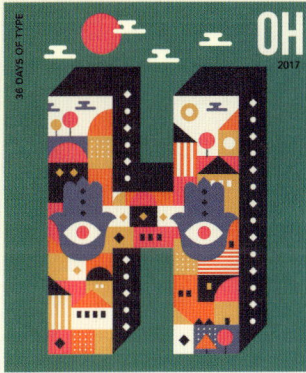

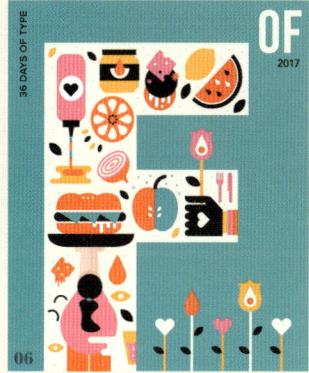

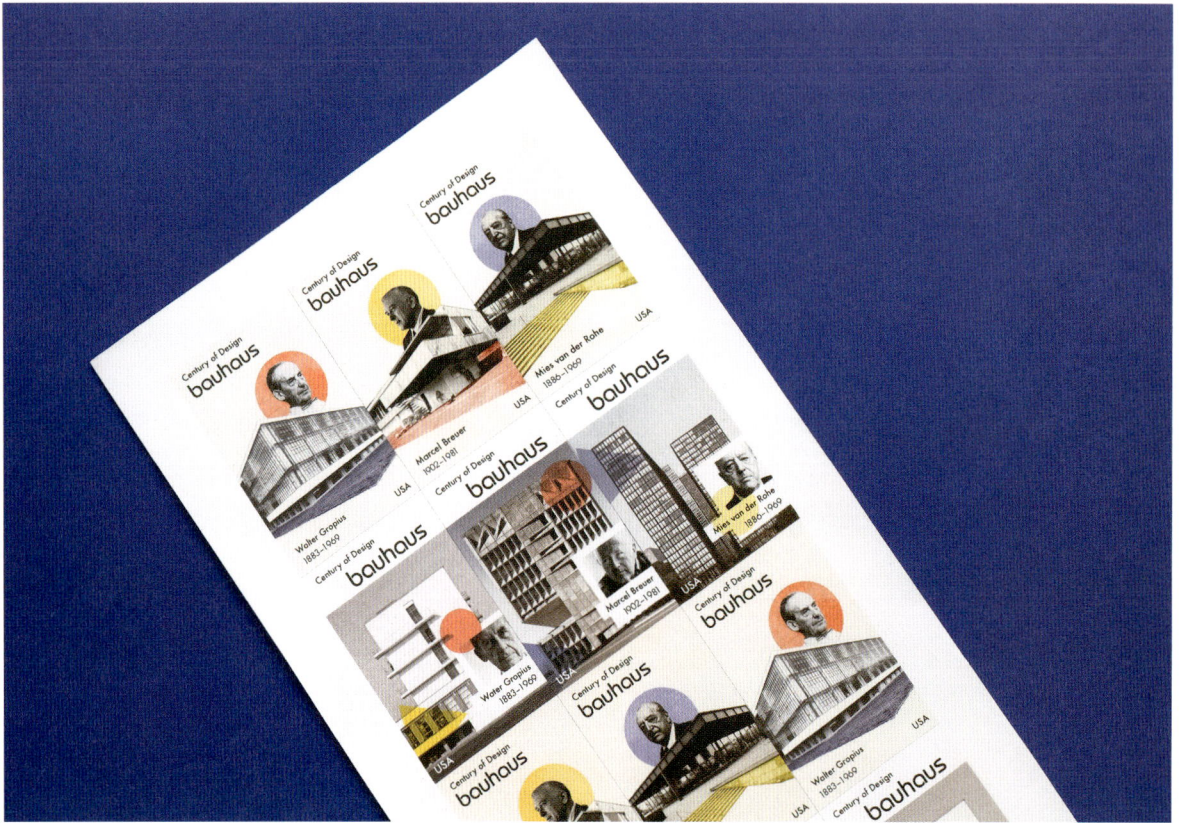

Bauhaus Stamp Design

Design: Ahyoon Kim
Photography: Paola Chen Li

The objective of this project was to create a cohesive design for stamps and brochures that represent the Bauhaus Movement and three of its architects— Walter Gropius, Mies van der Rohe and Marcel Breuer. The overall design utilizes simple shapes, primary colors and the geometric typography, Futura, following the Bauhaus style. Information about the movement and those three Bauhaus architects are written on both the brochures and information cards.

Century of Design
bauhaus

1919 - 1933

Walter Gropius 1883 - 1969

As a founder and director of the Bauhaus, Walter Gropius tried to combine art and design and built the famous Bauhaus Dessau building. After he moved to the US, he taught at the Harvard Graduate School of Design. He is regarded as one of the pioneers of modern architecture.

Marcel Breuer 1902 - 1981

Marcel Breuer was originally a student at the Bauhaus and later became a master carpenter. He was famous for his invention of tubular steel furniture. After he moved to New York, he continued his career in architecture, working on numerous projects including the Whitney Museum.

Mies van der Rohe 1886 - 1969

Mies van der Rohe was appointed as the last director of the Bauhaus. After his emigration to the US, he also became the head of the architectural school at the Illinois Institute of Technology in Chicago. His architectural style is known for its clarity and simplicity.

The Bauhaus
1919 - 1933

Mies van der Rohe
1886 - 1969

Second Director of the Bauhaus

"Less is more."

Postage Stamps

Design: Ilia Savonkin

During the creation of a brand identity for a winery, Ilia Savonkin came up with an idea to design a series of postage stamps related to France, Spain and Italy.

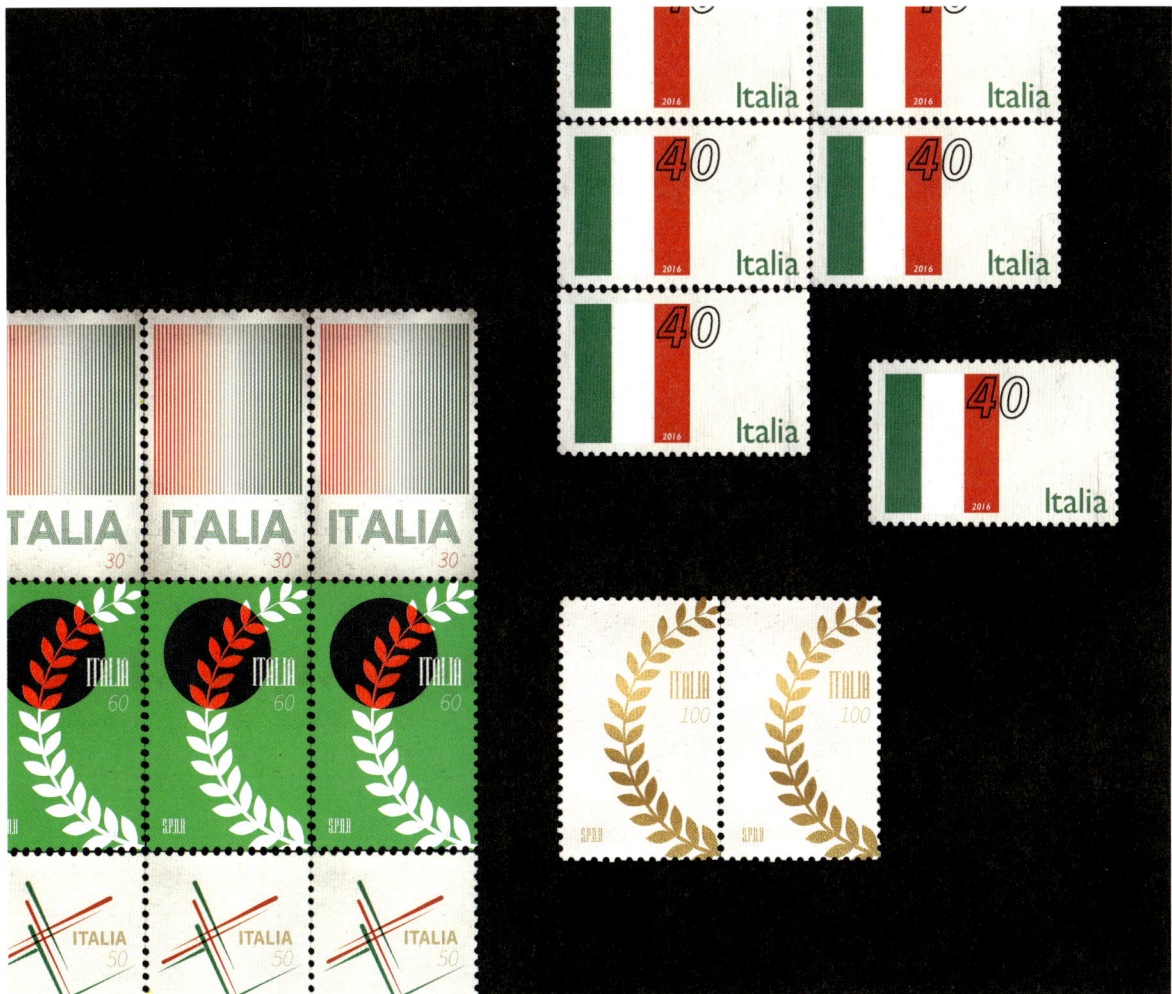

Robin Boyd—
Commemorative Stamp
Collection 2019

Design: Thomas O'Brien

2019 marked the centenary of the birth of Robin Boyd, a highly respected and influential Australian architect based in Melbourne, Victoria. This collection of stamps provides abstract-illustrative representations of four significant buildings designed by Boyd throughout his career. These stamps graphically represent modernist concepts and aesthetics with the use of geometric shapes and a minimal color palette. The use of "100¢" portrays 100 years since his birth.

Modernist World Stamps

Design: Youri V. Kiangala

This modernist stamp design for Brazil, Peru, Congo DR and Belgium is part of Youri V. Kiangala's project started in 2018. Youri got inspiration from research about modernist designers, such as Wim Crouwel and their ways of working. Using his new knowledge, Youri designed stamps for different countries worldwide.

Personal Identity

Design: Evan Wijaya

This project was an expression of Evan Wijaya's interests and personality. It consisted of various types of paper ephemera, such as vintage tickets, tags, labels and stamps. The stamps express his beliefs about the certain aspects of life. The name "Evan" can be roughly translated as "young warrior." And warriors from different cultures represent Evan's interests and are translated into the stamp design.

⁰¹Pater noster, qui es in caelis, sanctificetur nomen tuum. ⁰²Adveniat regnum tuum. Fiat voluntas tua, sicut in caelo, et in terra.

EVAN WIJAYA

Game of Thrones Stamp Design

Design: Nazlıcan Turan

The final season of *Game of Thrones*, one of the most popular series of recent times, aired in 2019. When Nazlıcan Turan was designing stamps, she chose the most famous cities in the series. She cut papers and put them on top of each other and created surfaces, then edited them on the computer.

STAMP DESIGNS · TAIWAN · LOWEI

KING'S LANDING

DRAGONSTONE

QARTH

WINTERFELL

THE WALL

Stamp for TSSM

Art Direction, Creative Direction and Design:
Dongrun Xie
Photography: Victory State Library

To represent Melbourne as an entity, Dongrun Xie depicted the youth of Melbourne because of the important role they play in the future development of the city. The children are a symbol of hope, to show Melbourne as an entity full of opportunities and potential. The yellow eight-pointed star and slogans symbolize Melbourne as a positive and rapidly growing city.

A Stamp for Christmas

Design: Cecilia Marzocchi
Client: Ufficio Filatelico e Numismatico
San Marino

Cecilia Marzocchi designed a stamp
for the Republic of San Marino. On the
stamp, the hands join together in the
same direction and display a symbol
of solidarity while forming the shape of
Christmas tree, reminiscent of Mount
Titan where San Marino was built. In
the background, the typical cableway is
carrying people and gifts to celebrate.
This stamp won first prize in the
competition held by Ufficio Filatelico
e Numismatico San Marino and was
officially released on September 26, 2017.

Explorers Club

Design Agency: Utopia
Design: Tamara Isles and Sean Creighton
Art Director: James Atkins

Explorers Club is a unique collection of accommodations paired with off-the-map expeditions. It required a refreshed identity to represent the uniqueness and exclusivity of the decade-old brand. Inspired by the humble postage stamp as a symbol of travel and exploration, Utopia created a collection of stamps to capture the spirit of each place. This eclectic identity provided a window into and captured its individuality.

RSA   EXPLORERS CLUB   *Tanda Tula*

ZIM   EXPLORERS CLUB   *Mana Pools*

Franschhoek — *Tuckie's* — EXPLORERS CLUB

Hermanus — *La Gratitude* — EXPLORERS CLUB

Franschhoek — *16 Cabriere Street* — EXPLORERS CLUB

Calitzdorp — *Daniels Kraal Farm* — EXPLORERS CLUB

Orange Free State — *The Prymsberg Estate* — EXPLORERS CLUB

Franschhoek — *Explorers Club* — EXPLORERS CLUB

Franschhoek — *Honeymoon Cottage* — EXPLORERS CLUB

Franschhoek — *Forest Cottages* — EXPLORERS CLUB

Franschhoek — *Cook's Cottage* — EXPLORERS CLUB

Kenya — *Shela Beach House* — EXPLORERS CLUB

Simonstown — *Littlehampton* — EXPLORERS CLUB

Franschhoek — *La Cotte House* — EXPLORERS CLUB

Townsquares

Design Agency: Makers Company

Makers Company always gets inspired by vintage ephemera, especially the craftsmanship in the humble postage stamp. They decided to create a digital illustration using Adobe Illustrator and Photoshop for each city they visited. This series consists of various cities and small towns. Makers Company wanted to pay tribute to two things they love: design and travel.

Pigalle

Design: Aurélien Jeanney

Aurélien Jeanney made this animated stamp project for fun. It was inspired by the magnificent basketball court in the Pigalle district, Paris. This was also the first step of Maison Tangible's Stamped Interview, a project in which Aurélien asked various artists to design a set of three stamps.

Slovenia—Country of Four Landscapes Stamp Collection

Design: Gregor Pogačnik

When exploring the motifs of the stamps for Slovenia, Gregor Pogačnik discovered that Slovenian traditions, food, monuments and holidays are often illustrated in the same unimaginative manner. Gregor challenged himself to represent these Slovenian characteristics in a simple, but visually interesting way. He chose Slovenia's impressive geographical diversity as the motif. And the final work consists of four illustrations— the coastline, hills, Alps and forests.

Flora and Fauna
Colombian Tribute

Design Agency: David Espinosa IDS

The design concept of this set of stamps, illustrations and packaging was inspired by the Colombian flora, fauna and pre-Columbian art, including the most characteristic animals and plants of Colombia.

FLOR DE CAYENA

COLIBRÍ

DELFÍN ROSADO

PASSIFLORA

NBA Stamp Collection

Design: Hongjian Li

Hongjian Li designed a stamp collection of NBA teams by exploring different abstract compositions with different colors and relevant elements of the basketball court, such as lines, circles, arcs and basket nets.

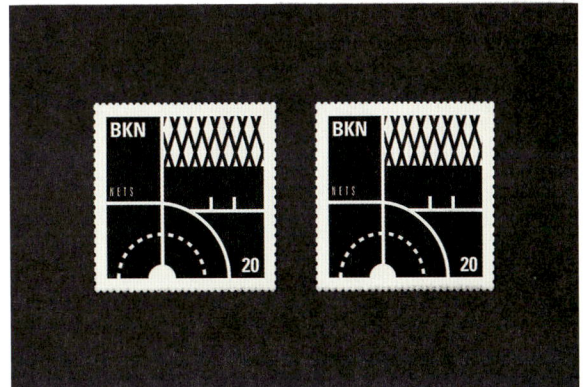

Winter Olympics Stamp

Design Agency: Graphasel Design Studio
Art Direction: Laszlo Ordogh
Design: Luca Hejja
Client: Hungarian Post
Photography: Luca Hejja

Cooperating with the Hungarian Olympic Committee, the Hungarian Post welcomed the 2018 Winter Olympics. The main motif of this commemorative stamp is the number 176 enclosed in a laurel wreath, which reflects the number of Olympic gold medals so far awarded to Hungarian athletes. Meanwhile, this stamp features an emerging Hungarian sport—short track speed skating. And the envelope represents the silhouette of a skier. This stamp was also the winner of the Hungarian Post's Art Award in 2019.

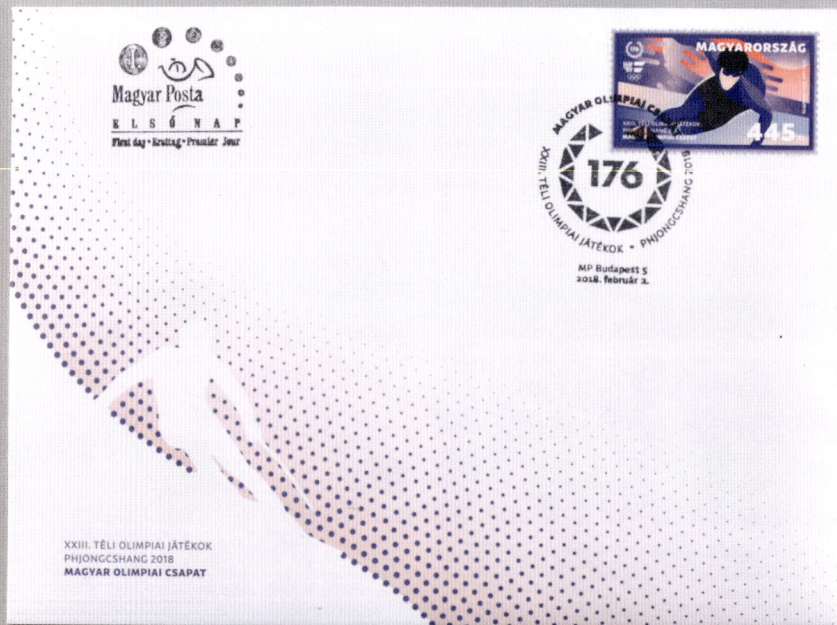

CHF 12.00

CHF 18.00

CHF 24.00

United Nations Definitive Stamp Series 2019

Concept and Illustration: Chris Gash
Design: Rorie Katz
Client: United Nations Postal Administration

Chris Gash designed this stamp series
for the global topics that concern the
United Nations—gender equality, sexual
exploitation and human migration.

The Calendar of
Unusual Holidays

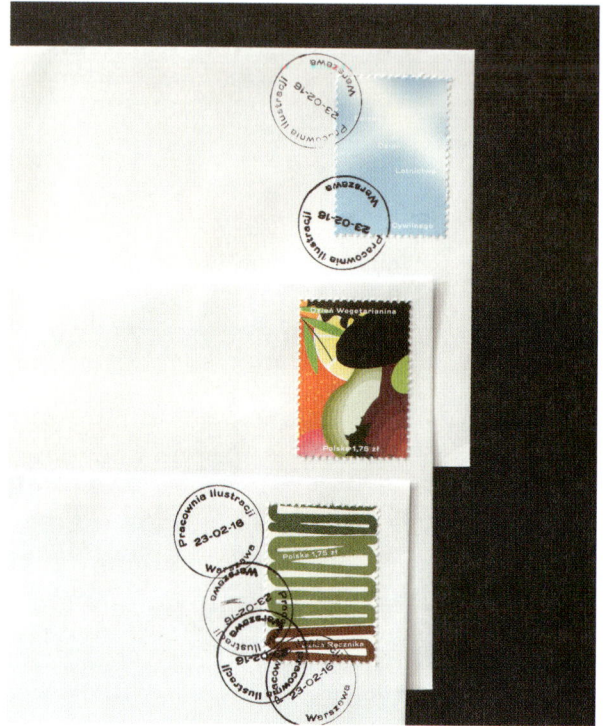

Design: Jacek Walesiak
Photography: Aleksandra Pavoni

The inspiration for this project was the visual designs of commemorative postage stamps in Poland. Jacek Walesiak states that such designs in the 1960s and 1980s were of higher quality. This project also commemorates unusual holidays that do not exist on official national calendars, such as Towel Day, Mushroom Day and Lighthouse Day. Altogether, 30 illustrations were created. The graphic form of the projects was meant to create a cohesive illustration in a set of stamps whilst remaining visually attractive in the form of a single stamp.

Dzień
Skarpetek
Polska
1,75 zł

Pracownia ilustracji
23-02-16
Warszawa
Dzień Ręcznika
Polska 1,75 zł

Historical Fire Truck
Postal Stamps

Design Agency and Illustration: Janz Design
Cooperation: designbüro behr

This series of stamps won second place
in the 2019 design contest "Postal Stamp
Series—Historical Fire Trucks" held by
the German Ministry of Finance in Berlin.
Janz Design tried to create something
new and went for simple illustrations of
fire trucks from three different eras and
made them look like plastic scale models.
They are designed not only for adults, but
for the younger generation.

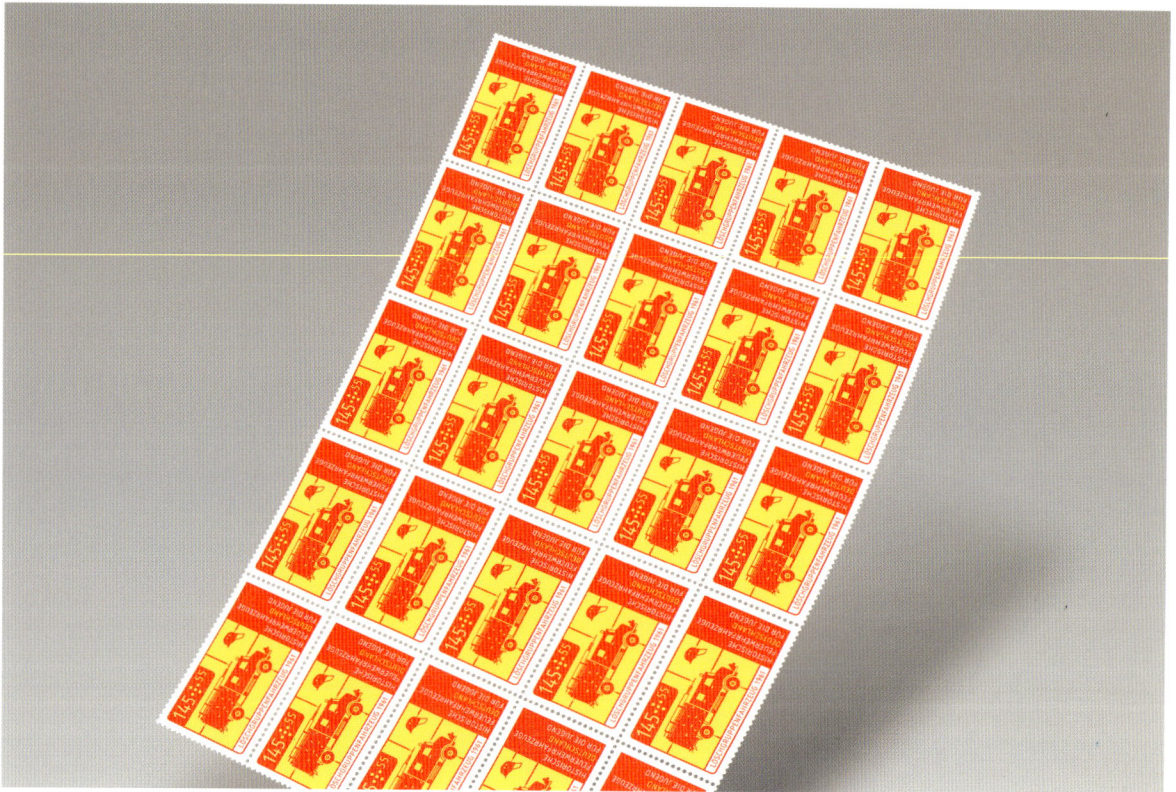

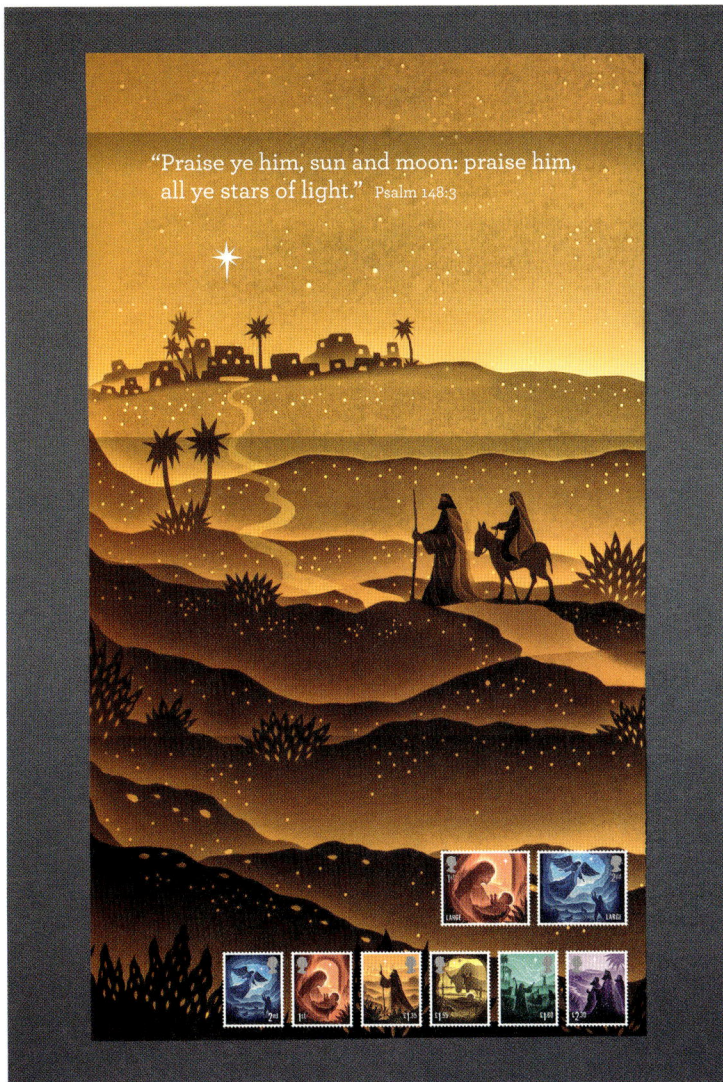

Royal Mail Christmas Stamps

Design Agency: Charlie Smith Design
Client: Royal Mail

Charlie Smith Design was asked to produce a Nativity-themed collection with a 3D style for the UK's Royal Mail Christmas collection. Working on such a small canvas created particular challenges and paper art seemed to be the most suitable approach to retain the details. The paper-cutting artist duo Hari and Deepti was a perfect choice. They typically work on large-scale A1 cutting projects, so scaling that down was a significant part of the creation. The final work is a set of intricate paper-art with jewel-like lighting to bring the magical story of Christmas to life.

You've Got Mail

Design: Cameron Haid

This series of postage stamps consists of elements of international tourism and symbols of different countries as well as a few inspirations from Cameron Haid's mind. Cameron refreshed his unsatisfied student project into a new style with bright colors, big typography and bold illustrations that can stand out on the corner of any envelope.

JAPAN 75
こんにちは

ISRAEL 20
2018
833-473

GERMANY
1918
CG22   1372
6860

LAX
Los Angeles
80
1965
003

UNITED
STATES
OF
AMERICA
099-293
2018
$2.00
USA ★

50
390-225
2018
KANSAS
USA

MONTANA
088-342
2018
* 50

GEORGIA 80
USA
80
2018

Flanders 1$

IRELAND $2

80
1950
NEDERLAND

PORTUGAL
500

Sierra
Nevada 50
USA

SAKURA 75
桜の花

CHUREITO 75
Japan
2018

Matterhorn 002
90

90¢ 2018
PATAGONIA

Alpine 50

1969 A05
3409
THE MOON

USA $2
HYDRO
ENERGY 2018

Stamps for the Anniversary of Athens School of Fine Arts

Design: Zofia Stybor
Cooperation: Athens School of Fine Arts
(ASFA) and Elta Hellenic Post (ELTA)

These stamps were designed by
Zofia Stybor during her exchange
with Erasmus Mundus in ASFA, with
the collaboration of ELTA—the Greek
official post company. After a few months
of discussion with ELTA's designer
and ASFA's graphic design professor
Alexandra Georgiadou, they created
a special series of stamps for the
anniversary of ASFA. Zofia was inspired
by the buildings of ASFA and the old
factory, and utilized the shapes and
characteristics of the Greek alphabet in
the stamps.

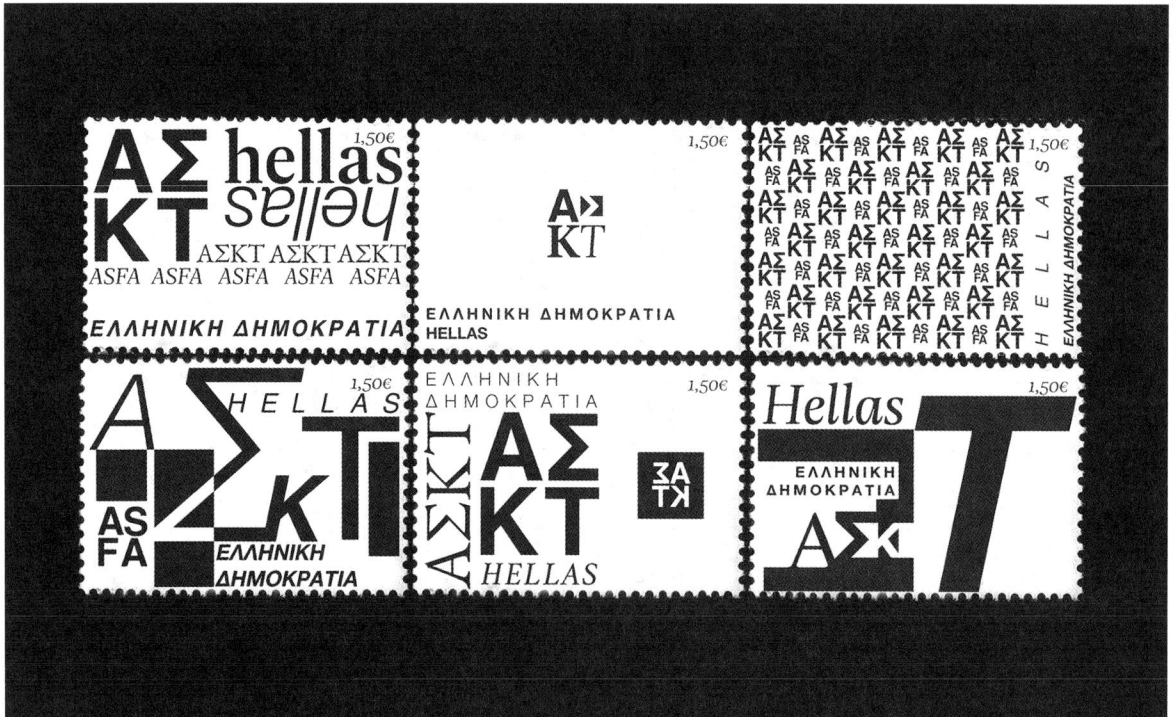

seals

A seal is a device for making an impression in clay, wax or other materials, originally used for authenticating a document or sealing an envelope. Historically, many seals were circular in design, while ovals and shield-shapes were also used. The elements of seal design were merged into the modern graphic design because of the seal's unique vintage style.

Kong Studio Branding

Design Agency: Kong Studio
Creative Direction: Kevin He

The logo is based on the Chinese character "kong." The word is commonly translated as "emptiness." "Kong" is the studio founder Kevin He's creative philosophy about spatial treatment. The Chinese character "kong" pervades the identity in various forms, such as stamping, and ranges from leitmotif to empty space as a monogram derived from Kevin He's initials, K.H.

Pinto—Travel Africa

Design Agency: Bureau Rabensteiner
Design: Mike Rabensteiner
Photography: Mike Rabensteiner

As a safari travel partner, Pinto provides customers with adventures in Africa's most sparsely populated countries. To supplement the logo, the "key to Africa" for stamping was designed. This supplement has a marvelous effect on printed materials. The "key to Africa" has many uses that can transmit a genuine and authentic feeling.

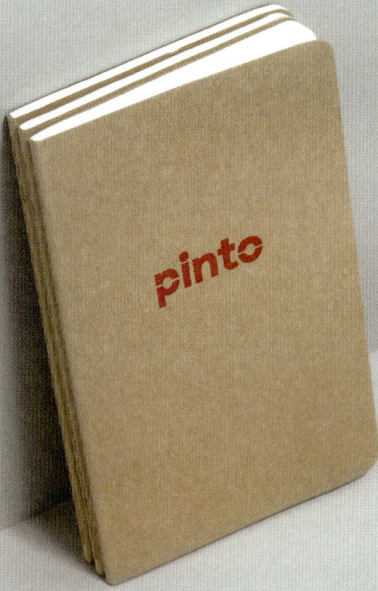

Andaluz

Design Agency: Plau, Poema
Art Direction: Eduardo Mattos
Creative Direction: Rodrigo Saiani and
Gustavo Saiani
Design: Luisa Borja, Juliana Valverde,
Eduardo Mattos and Caio Vaccaro

Andaluz is a Brazilian audio and video production company. Their name was inspired by the surrealist short film, *An Andalusian Dog*, directed by Luis Buñuel—a gritty and non-linear experimentation in filmmaking. In order to echo such an inspiration, the designers created a rocking chair with a combination of a horse head and letter A. The stamps used on sharp yellow paper are widely used in the stationery.

La Bodeguilla

Design: Enrique Presa
Cooperation: Maggy Villarroel
Photography: Miquel Torres

La Bodeguilla is a restaurant located at the center of Palma de Mallorca, Spain and founded in 1986. This design took the stencil style of the fonts formerly used for marking the wine barrels as inspiration. Likewise, the use of wood, the engraving and the rubber stamp reminds customers of the world of wine and craft.

Major Tom

Design Agency:
JEROME AND ZIMMERMAN

The design concept of Major Tom consists of the aesthetics of the secret society, the Illuminati. The elegance given by the metal engravings is remarkable. Meanwhile, the visual impact in contrast with the cotton paper is simply spectacular. The printed and engraved copper creates an effect of something ancient, but with a formal institutional look.

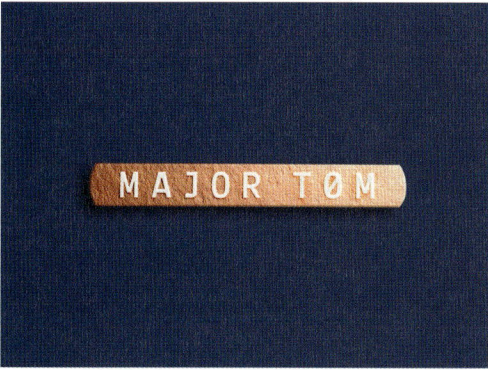

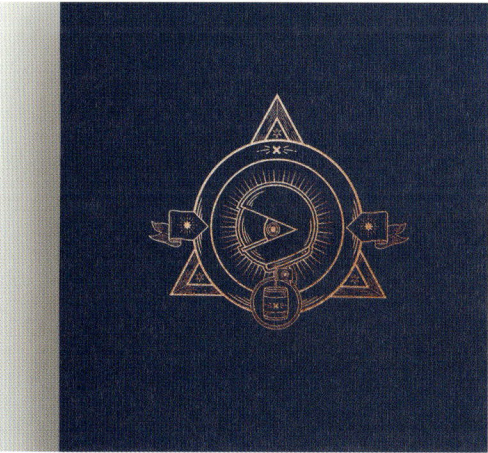

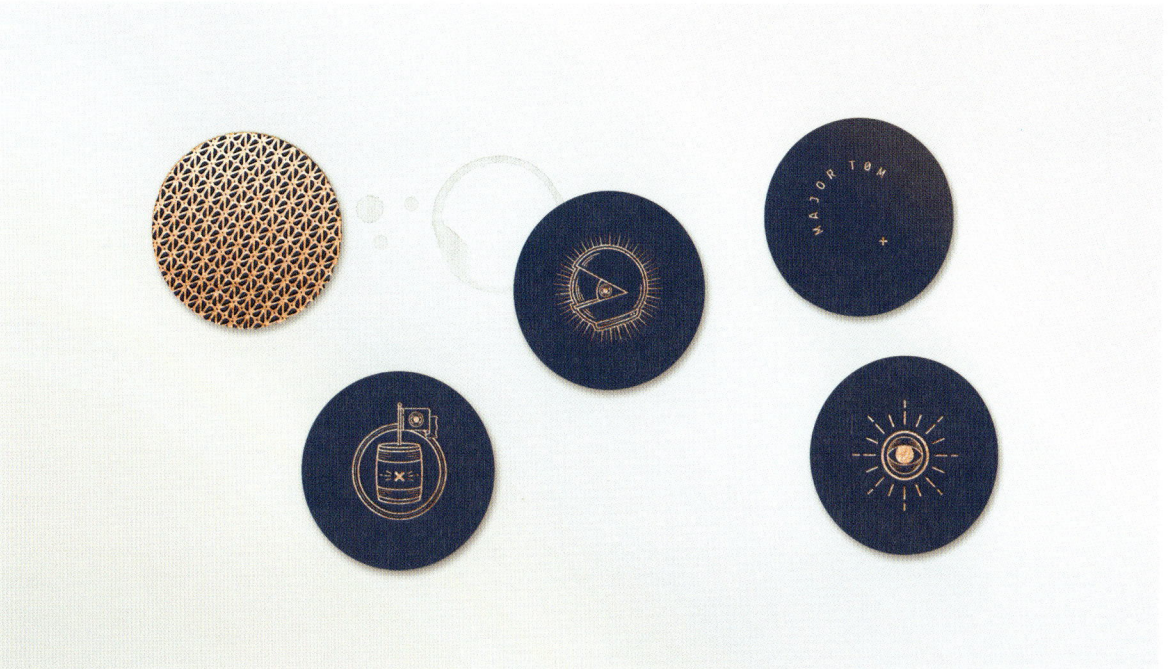

Vins Nomades

Illustration and Design:
Alexandre Mercier

Vins Nomades is a wine import agency based in Ottawa, Canada. Alexandre Mercier used a vintage style for this branding. And the hexagonal stamping makes the brand remarkable.

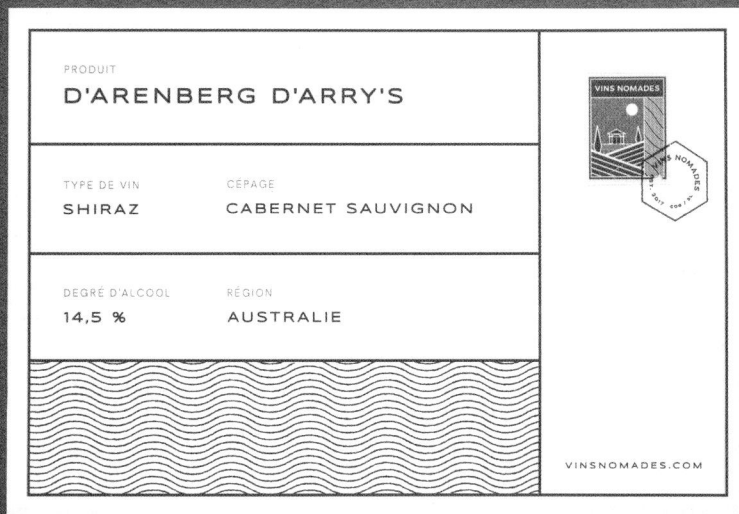

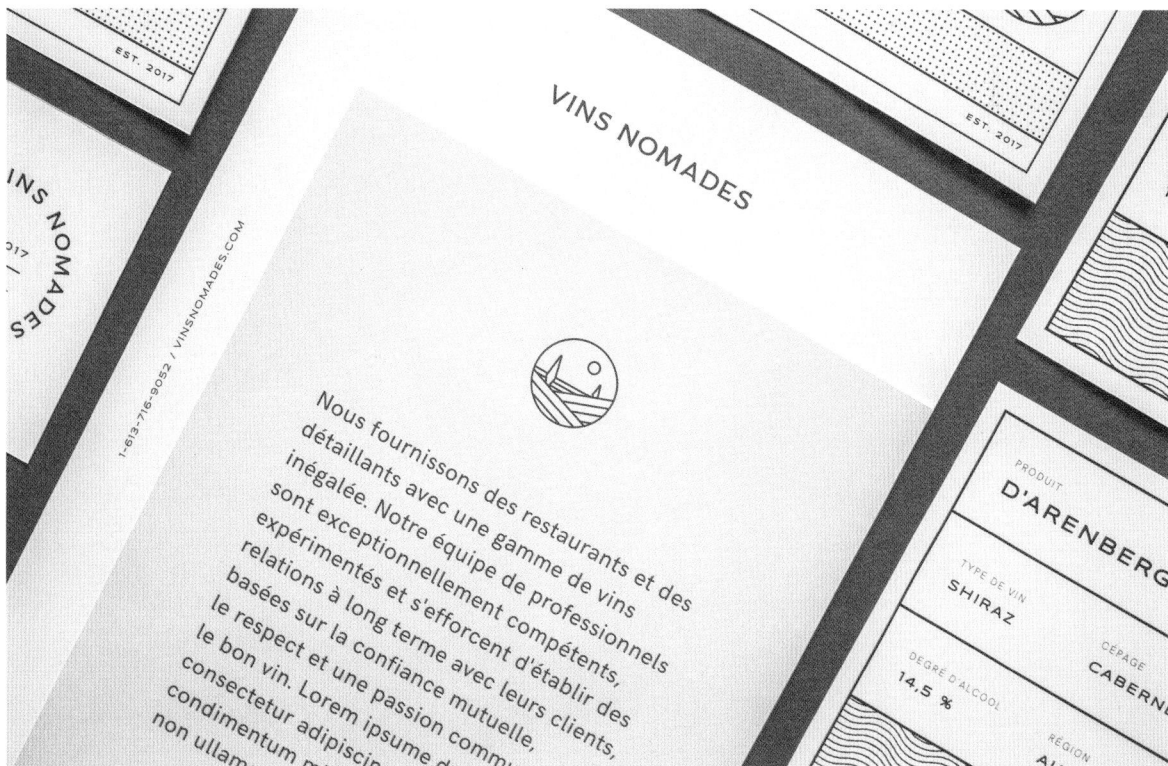

Katenitza

Design Agency: Marka Collective
Client: Katenitza
Photography: Marka Collective

Katenitza is a startup company that makes handcrafted ceramic tiles. The logo represents one of their most emblematic shapes combined with the hand—a symbol of uniqueness and personal touch. It also alludes to Hamsa—a well-known symbol of home protection, blessings, power, and strength. Marka Collective made a lot of traditional wooden stamps with blind embossing and using of pliers. The stamps became a great combination of hand-made quality and personal touch.

KATENITZA

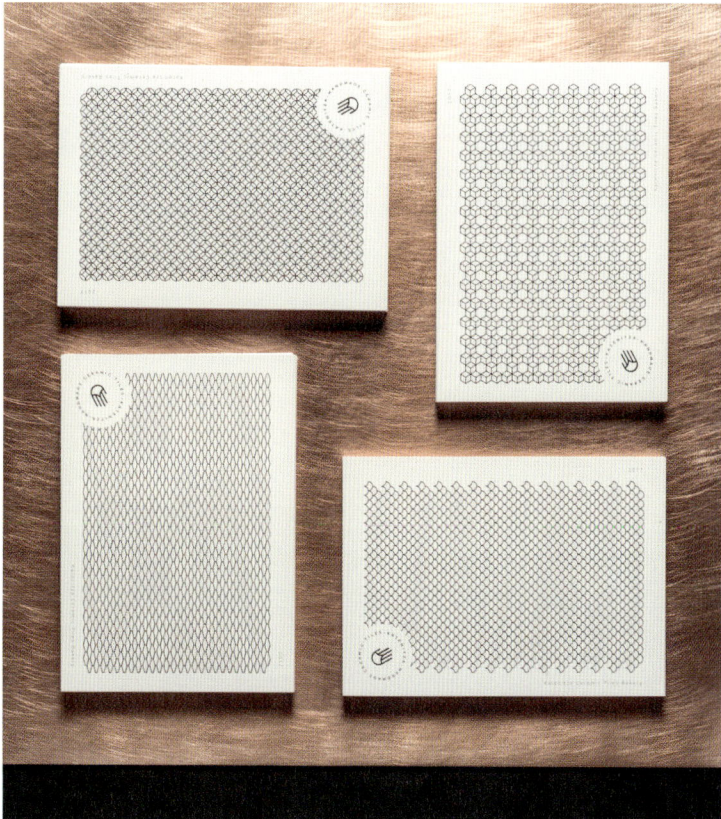

Pimiento Argentino Grill

Design Agency: Blürbstudio
Photography: Matt Wojnar

Pimiento is a well-known restaurant serving Argentinean beef specialties in Kraków, Poland. The reason Blürbstudio chose traditional printing forms and high-quality paper was to give the customers an opportunity to feel that they are enjoying a premium service. Blürbstudio used envelopes and wax seals to put an emphasis on a tradition, craft and a personalized image. And it is a sensual experience when customers need to break the seal, open the envelope, hear the sound of the seal crush and feel its subtle structure under their fingertips.

Stories of Italy

Art Direction: Massimo Pitis and
Federica Marziale Iadevaia
Graphic Design: Federica Marziale
Iadevaia (Pitis e associati)
Client: Stories of Italy
Photography: Claudio Fabbro

Stories of Italy is a duo of creative artists, Matilde
Antonacci and Dario Buratto, in Milan. To echo
that they work in typical Italian craft traditions,
Federica Marziale Iadevaia built a unique visual
identity with the element of traditional stamping.

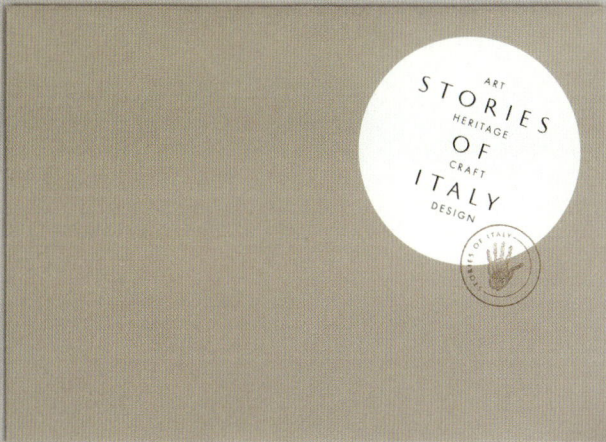

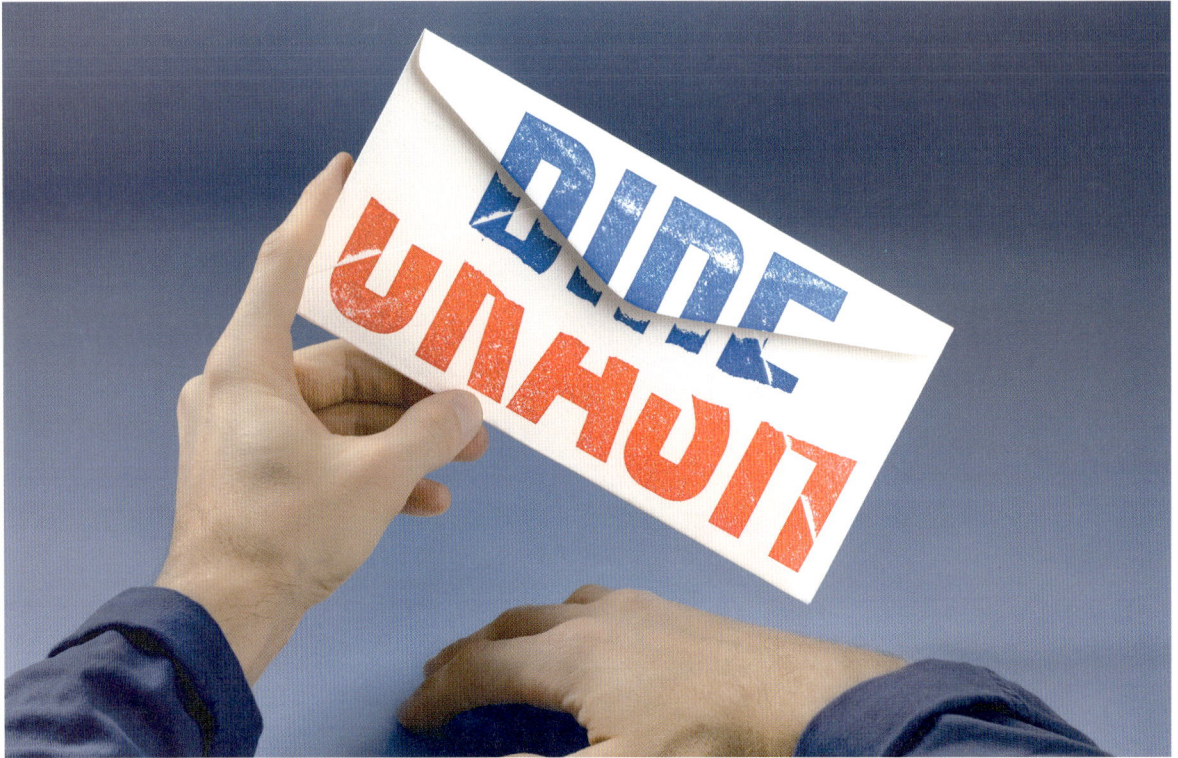

Ride & Crash

Design Agency and Art Direction:
Lundgren+Lindqvist
Photography: Carl Oliver Ander

The video game startup Ride & Crash asked Lundgren+Lindqvist for a full visual identity. The two words in the company's name represent opposites and reflect the characteristics of the two founders. The two words of the name have seemingly crashed into each other, removing chunks of the bottom of "RIDE" in cool blue and the top of "CRASH" in fiery red, respectively. Like pieces of a jigsaw puzzle, the two halves become one and belong together even when they drift apart.

Power-nap Over Design Studio Branding

Design Agency: Power-nap Over
Design Studio
Design: Vita Mak

Power-nap Over Design Studio injected their design ideas onto stationery that they use to get in touch with their clients and friends. The rubber stamp enhances the aesthetics of the visual identity, while it delivers warmth to the addressees.

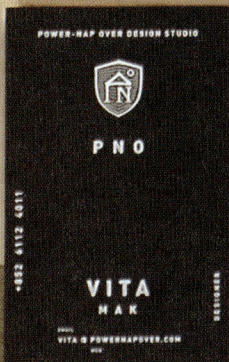
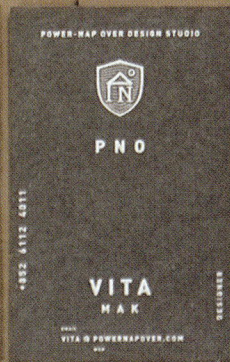
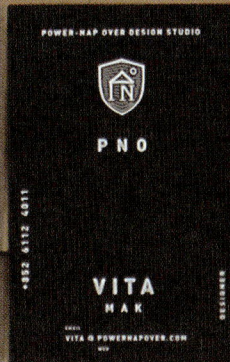

Visual Identity for Polish National Parks

Design: Sylvia Baosh
Image Source: Freepik.com

The visual identity of Polish national parks is an environmentally friendly project that was inspired by wycinanki—the art of Polish paper cutting. It tries to adapt the Polish national parks to the sustainable and flexible concepts of the world today. Stampings play an important role in the project as they serve as a record of visits to each park. The collecting of these stampings can be one of the enjoyments for potential travelers. And those visits also can raise people's awareness of environmental preservation.

Picasso Educa

Design Agency: pfp, disseny
Client: Picasso Museum

pfp, disseny was asked to design the
brochure for the educational program
of the Picasso Museum in Barcelona for
children of all ages. They did not want to
create a childish image for the brochure
and they used rubber stamps to show the
creativity and charm of handiwork.

P4:
Hola Picass
Va començar
acabar pinta

P5:
Retrats de P
Aprenem d'a
de com Pica
Hola Picass
Va començar
acabar pinta

E

a manera
d'aquest gènere.

des a les
brir-les i
"llegir-lo".

nverteixen

P

5

DÀRIA I **BATXILLERAT**

2N QUADRIMESTRE
De l'1 de febrer al 21 de juny

VISITA A SALES:
DIÀLEG DAVANT DE L'OBRA
Visita per cinc obres de la col·lecció, on es promou l'atenció del grup sencer a través de la reflexió sobre les seves opinions i les dels seus companys.

Picasso descobreix París Novetat!
Veiem obres del Musée d'Orsay que van influenciar al jove Picasso.
Retrats de Picasso
Família, amics i coneguts, a través de la particular òptica de l'artista.
Diverses tècniques de Picasso
Un pintor que també feu escultura, dibuix, gravat, ceràmica...
La revolució de l'art
Al segle xx, Picasso va canviar totalment el paper i el significat de l'art.

VISITA A SALES I TALLER
Els diferents Picassos Nou taller!
Un artista que era molts artistes a l'hora i per a qui pintar era un acte de llibertat.
Paisatges Novetat!
Mirem el món, la natura i la ciutat a través dels ulls de Picasso, i explorem com representar-los. Per 1r i 2n d'ESO.
T'ha sortit calcat
Explorarem el concepte del retrat i l'autoretrat, i com ens veiem els uns als altres.

VISITA A SALES:
DIÀLEG DAVANT DE L'OBRA
Retrats de Picasso
Família, amics i coneguts, a través de l'òptica particular de l'artista.
Diverses tècniques de Picasso
Un pintor que també feu escultura, dibuix, gravat, ceràmica...
La revolució de l'art
Al segle xx, Picasso va canviar totalment el paper i el significat de l'art.

Sm

Luxembourg Branding and Packaging

Design: Jasmina Zornic

Luxembourg is a pastry shop in Belgrade, Serbia. Jasmina Zornic wanted to create a completely new feeling for this brand. Because the package is an important connection between Luxembourg and its consumers, Jasmina created seals and stamps that depict the tastes and products of the bakery. The consumers can choose and buy their favorites pastries, then put them into the to-go boxes and decorate them with seals and stamps.

LUXEMBOURG
Ice-cream & Cakes
Nevesinjska 12, 11000 Beograd
+38160 016 28 56, 011 5633 262

LUXEMBOURG
2016
CAKES
LUXEMBOURG

LUXEMBOURG
2016
ICE CREAMS
LUXEMBOURG

Innpromenade Kufstein

Design Agency: Aberjung GmbH
Photography: Aberjung GmbH

Studio Aberjung in East Tyrol, Austria
is small, but perfectly formed agency.
It established its roots in product and
graphic design. The fabulously beautiful
natural surroundings in the heart of the
Lienz Dolomites inject Aberjung's work
with the essential spirit of authenticity.

inn
prome
nade.
Wohnen am Inn.
ÖSTERREICH
68
Wohnen
(Er)leben
innpromenade
Mitten
im Grünen,
direkt
am Inn.
WWW.INNPROMENADE.AT

WOHNEN
(ER)LEBEN
L(I)EBEN
KUFSTEIN
20
16
INNPROMENADE

XI WU Mooncake

Design Agency: Leaping Creative
Design Direction: Zen Zheng
Design: Qilin Huang and Weikang Liu
Photography: DALI

The design of the XI WU Mooncake is an integration of unadorned traditional woodblock printing craftsmanship and contemporary design style, aiming at digging and demonstrating the meanings in ordinary daily objects. With the coordination of Mooncake's molding, packages and a set of wooden stamps as a gift box, XI WU Mooncake provides a unique experience of seeing, opening, eating and having fun.

The Ol' Box

Design: Tiago Sá

In 2018, the Ol' box, an online business selling antique coins, asked Tiago Sá to renew their visual identity. Tiago Sá decided to create a single sheet of paper and stampings of Ol' Box's logo and relevant shipping information. Meanwhile, Tiago Sá designed a thank-you card where someone can stamp the logo on one side and write something with a gold ink pen on the other side.

Filidoro—Argentinian Brewery

The brewery Filidoro asked Tricota Agency for a brand update. Tricota Agency followed up on Filidoro's handcrafted process of brewing beer and developed a new, handmade brand. They explored many ways to express Filidoro's spirit, such as doing sketches of both the name and the rooster. And they finally created a warm, home-made feeling.

Design Agency: Tricota Agency
Client: Filidoro

Print and Space

Design: Daniele Simonelli
Copywriting: Daniele Movarelli
Printing: NostroInchiostro
Photography: Alessandro Campisi

Print and Space represents a mapping of the solar system involving techniques and processes that include the art of printing. In order to give this project a sense of mystery and ancient knowledge, Daniele Simonelli designed an envelope printed with gold hot foil and closed it with a custom wax seal that highlights the project's logo.

Jacqueline Fleury

Art Direction and Graphic Design:
Sylvain Toulouse

Jacqueline Fleury is a talented seamstress who specializes in creating custom drapery. Using illustrations of the tools and Jacqueline's identity with retro-style, Sylvain Toulouse created a traditional craftsmanship flavor. The custom logo stamping provides a classic way to seal envelopes with wax. The pastel-colored palette adds a delicate, feminine touch to the brand.

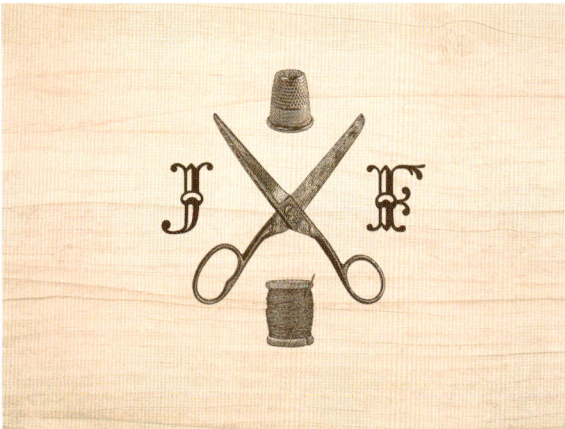

Kowloon Buffet Dim Sum Restaurant

Design Agency: Quan+Duong
Illustration: Ha-Duong Nguyen
Design: Tri-Quan Duong and Ha-Duong Nguyen

Kowloon Restaurant is a Hong Kong-style Chinese dim sum buffet and hot pot restaurant in Hanoi, Vietnam. As the red lantern is easily spotted on the street in Hong Kong, China, it's regarded as the key visual. The stamping is used to make a mark on the tissue as well as on the carry-out packages in order to add extra value to the brand itself. The ink mark gives the consumers a feeling that fits the overall mood and tone of the brand.

Roboost—Powered in Hell

Design Agency: INVADE
Photography: @gioup

Roboost is a coffee brand in Brooklyn. The first step of design was the naming proposal. INVADE came up with a portmanteau—roboost, blending the coffee bean robusta and its effect of power-boosting. Inspired by New York City's sub-cultures and robusta's characteristics, INVADE adopted the brand concept "powered in hell" with a devil drawn in an urban style. To highlight the brand's main role, INVADE developed an easily-produced label by using stamping, which makes the brand look strong and streetwise.

TAPEA

Design Agency: David Espinosa IDS

The culinary enterprise TAPEA asked David Espinosa IDS to develop a visual identity. Based on a logo with series of accessories, the identity shows various pictograms. The typeface is in a typewriter style and they use a color palette with Mediterranean colors, such as red and green accompanied by gold. Together, they reflect the tradition, experience and quality of Spanish food in a new and innovative way.

THE LAND
THE BEST OF THE SPANISH MOUNTAINS
WEEKLY GASTRONOMIC SELECTIONS OF THE LAND:
TO FINISH
THE BEST OF SPANISH PASTRY ENTRANCES

THE SEA
THE BEST OF THE SPANISH MARITIME COASTS

TO START
THE BEST OF TRADITIONAL SPANISH GASTRONOMY
THE SEA
THE BEST
·TRADITIONAL SANGRÍA
8,50
11,90

Valletta VLT 1130,
Madrid.
+(91) 314 847 8541
general_office@tapea.com
Carrer de Dinamarca,
3-5 46240 Carlet,
Valencia.
+(91) 314 847 8545
leaders_office@tapea.com
INTERNATIONAL HOTEL PURPLE COAST
Nantes - France
4/12/2018
Estamos encantados de darle la bienvenida como nuevo distribuidor selecto de Tapea Internacional.
Nos sentimos honrados de que nos haya elegido para ayudarle con sus necesidades y estamos ansiosos
de estar a su disposición.
SPANISH GASTRONOMIC TRADITION
PASSION INNOVATION RESPECT
1939
www.tapea.com
TAPEA
SPANISH GASTRONOMIC TRADITION
PASSION
INNOVATION
RESPECT

Paula Simó

Art Direction and Creative Direction: Yinsen
Graphic Design: Lorena Sayavera and
María Pradera
Photography: Lorena Sayavera

Yinsen designed the identity for Paula Simó who has extensive experience in regional tourism, cultural and musical projects. Each of these stamps is manually stamped on the stationery, creating a unique and personalized visual identity with a language that can grow in the future.

seal GRAPHICS

I nspired by vintage seals, designers can now digitally render seal graphics for their personal or commissioned projects. The following collection showcases seal graphics used for branding, editorials and packaging.

1

2

3

4

5

6

7

8

9

10

11

12

13

14

15

16

1

2

3

4

5

6

7

8

KO!

9

BARBECUE
SAUCE
THAT PACKS
PUNCH!

10

Angry

ESTD 2003

KANGAROO
BOTTLED IN
KANSAS CITY
MISSOURI

11

AK

12

BARBECUE SAUCE WITH A PUNCH!

A K

13

ANGRY KANGAROO
BOTTLED IN KANSAS CITY, MISSOURI
BARBECUE CO.

14

BARBECUE SAUCE WITH A PUNCH!

15

THE
ONLY
BARBECUE
SAUCE
THAT PACKS
A
PUNCH

16

1

2

3

4

5

6

7

TASTE A FLAVOUR
AMERICAN
RESTAURANT & BBQ
A
OKLAHOMA CITY

8

ORIGINAL STYLE FROM
MARCINERY
HIGH QUALITY
TEES AND JACKETS

9

ESTD 2018
EAGLEWING
BARBERQUE
TRD · CSCO · MRK
ALWAYS SERVE WITH LOVE

10

AN ORIGINAL DEER HUNTER
REG 2019
TRADEMARK ESTABLISHED
PORTSMOUTH
UNITED KINGDOM
ESTD 2019

11

20 BLACK 19
AMPLIFIER
JAKARTA INDONESIA
—PASIFIC PLACE—

12

AMERICAN SIGN PAINTING
MAGE
THUNDER
UNITED STATES
OREGON
ORIGINAL STYLE

13

EST. 2013
EAGLEGASM
COMMUNITY
CINTAI BURUNGMU
KEDIRI, INA.

1

INTRODUCING
ESTD 2018   KEDIRI EAST
DUTCHY
VINTAGE FONT FAMILY & ILLUSTRATIONS
PROUDLY PRESENT BY
CRAFT SUPPLY CO

2

VINTAGE UNIFORM
BACKYARDIGANS
TRD MRK
VINTAGE UNIFORM

3

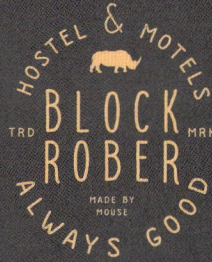

HOSTEL & MOTELS
TRD   MRK
BLOCK
ROBER
MADE BY MOUSE
ALWAYS GOOD

4

CRAFT SUPPLY CO
VINTAGE &
RETRO DESIGN
HANDCRAFTED STYLE
MADE IN KEDIRI
INDONESIA

5

PUT YOUR HEART MIND AND SOUL
ROTTERYN
EAST   JAVA

6

WEREWOLF
THE BEAST ONE
ESTD 2018
COLORADO
UNITED STATES
768990

7

EST. 1997
R
RUSTIC PINE FORTUNE

8

NO ROAD IS TOO LONG

EST · 1975

WHEN YOU HAVE GOOD COMPANY

⚡ BRONX GARAGE ⚡

9

EST. · 1976

LOOK DEEP INTO NATURE

SUMMER CAMP SEASON

10

WARUNG PAK SOLEH

SATE KOBRA

1995

CITA RASA TETAP TERJAGA TURUN TEMURUN

11

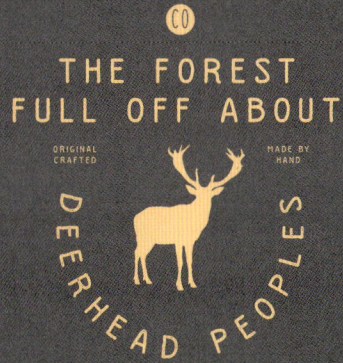

THE FOREST FULL OFF ABOUT

ORIGINAL CRAFTED · MADE BY HAND

DEERHEAD PEOPLES

12

INTRODUCING

ESTD 2018 · KEDIRI EAST

DUTCHY

VINTAGE FONT FAMILY & ILLUSTRATIONS
PROUDLY PRESENT BY:
CRAFT SUPPLY CO

13

CRAFT SUPPLY CO

VINTAGE & RETRO DESIGN

HANDCRAFTED STYLE

MADE IN KEDIRI
INDONESIA

14

VINTAGE UNIFORM

BACKYARDIGANS®

TRD MRX

VINTAGE UNIFORM

15

A WOLF LIVES HIS LIFE BY HIS OWN RULES
E S T BECAUSE THE RULES MAKE 0 1 8
US WIN
ORIGINAL HAND MADE
&.CO

1

RUN
OR BE ®
PREYED ON

2

TELL THEM THE NORTH REMEMBER
TRD MRK
• ARYA STARK •

3

WOLF . GANG
HAND MADE
NO 03
PASSION
MADE

4

FROM NATURE
FOR US

5

THE WILD IS NOT A LUXURY
TRD MRK
BUT A CITY THAT IS
IMPORTANT FOR THE
ESTD HUMAN SOUL 1987

6

THE MOUNTAINS ARE CALLING AND I MUST GO
9°C
DOWNTOWN ALASKA
NO.003-018.AV

7

WOLF WARRIOR TERROR
FANGS ALL OVER
THE WORLD

8

WOLF GANG TYPE
Trademark

9

THE WOLVES WILL COME AGAIN
TRADE 19 87 MARK
I AM A WOLF AND I WILL
NOT BE AFRAID
Arya Stark

10

1987
INTO THE WILD

11

·THE·
YOUNG
WOLF
1987

12

&.CO
TRD MRK
I NOW WALK INTO
THE WILD

13

19 87
FISHING AND ADVENTURE
SUPPLY.CO

14

WOLF SQUAD
8 7
INDUSTRY

15

LEAVE ONE WOLF ALIVE
TRD MRK
AND THE SHEEP ARE
NEVER SAFE

16

1

2

3

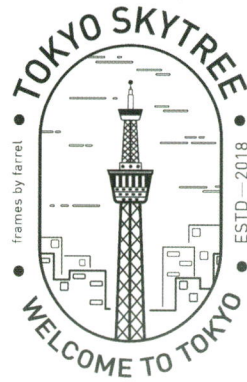

4

5

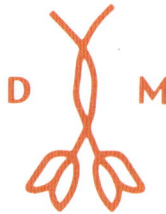

6

7

8

9

10

11

12

13

14

15

1

2

3

4

5

6

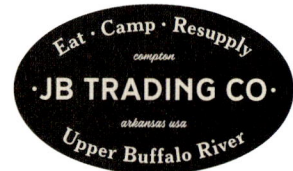

7

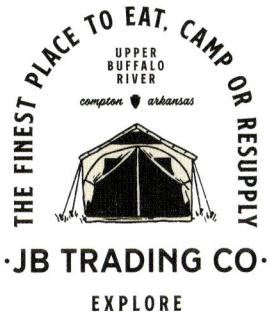

THE FINEST PLACE TO EAT, CAMP OR RESUPPLY

UPPER
BUFFALO
RIVER

compton • arkansas

·JB TRADING CO·

EXPLORE

8

JB TRADING CO

ARK   USA

Upper Buffalo River

9

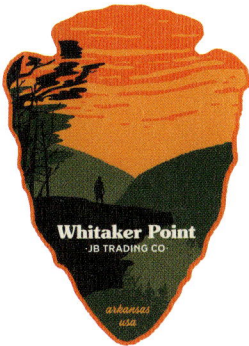

Whitaker Point
·JB TRADING CO·

arkansas
usa

10

JB TRADING CO

ARK   USA

Upper Buffalo River

11

Steel Creek
·JB TRADING CO·

12

JB TRADING CO

ARK   USA

Upper Buffalo River

13

1

2

3

4

5

6

7

8

9

10

11

12

13

14

15

16

17

1

2

3

4

5

6

7

8

Index

(shame-on-you)office

(shame-on-you)office (AKA S-O-Y) was founded by Ray and Rose, two graduates from the London College of Communication. The duo has spent time living and working in London, Shanghai, Taiwan and they're currently based on Xiamen Island. They have experience in graphic design, publication, exhibition curating, product design and other creative works.

behance.net/shame-on-you-office

Aberjung GmbH

Studio Aberjung in East Tyrol, Austria is small, but perfectly formed. It established its roots in product and graphic design. The fabulously beautiful natural surroundings in the heart of the Lienz Dolomites inject into Aberjung's work the essential spirit of authenticity.

aberjung.com

Ahyoon Kim

Ahyoon Kim is a Korean multi-disciplinary designer who lives in New York City. She received her bachelor of fine arts degree in graphic design from the Savannah College of Art and Design. Her work includes print media, packaging, branding, illustration and motion graphics.

ahyoonkim.com

Alexander Kuliev

Alexander Kuliev is a Moscow-based, independent graphic designer.

behance.net/hAck-Nolev

Alexandre Mercier

Alexandre Mercier is a graphic designer who mainly works in web design. He has begun a transition towards illustration, branding and cultural design. His approach is to experiment with typography, illustration and collage. Other passions that help fuel his works are visual arts, photography and music.

alexandremercier.com

Allons-y Alonso

Audrey Colombié is a graphic designer and artisan based in France. In her small design studio, Allons-y Alonso, she likes to play with paper, and give it language and emotion.

allonsyalonso.fr

Atelier1234567890

Atelier1234567890 is an art direction studio. It creates original concepts for cultural institutions and private partners in the fields of art, culture, luxury and music.

atelier1234567890.com

Aurélien Jeanney

Aurélien Jeanney is a French art director and multidisciplinary designer. He works with various media such as posters, typography, books, and motion design. Meanwhile, he runs a publishing house and gallery called Maison Tangible where they promote emerging design through exhibitions, meetings and public workshops with international artists.

aurelienjeanney.fr

Axter Chu Chon Kit

Axter Chu Chon Kit was born in Macau, China. He graduated from the department of art and creative design at Hsuan Chuang University. He is fond of illustration and typography.

behance.net/axterzinho

Balmer Hählen

Founded in 2011 by Priscilla Balmer and Yvo Hählen in the heartland of Lausanne, Switzerland, Balmer Hählen regularly receives awards in Switzerland and abroad. Their posters have been selected and exhibited several times in international competitions. Balmer Hählen is also distinguished by the quality of its prints.

balmerhahlen.ch

Blürbstudio

Blürbstudio helps define new brands, and reshapes and develops those that already exist. They create visual identities and translate them into the language of print and the Internet.

blurbstudio.com

Bruch—Idee & Form

Bruch—Idee & Form is a nationally and internationally awarded design studio based in Graz, Austria. They develop visual design concepts and strategies in the fields of branding, editorial design, packaging and signage.

studiobruch.com

Bureau Rabensteiner

Bureau Rabensteiner is a branding and graphic design studio based in Innsbruck, Austria. They do everything from branding to packaging for products ranging from books to bottles and for clients big and small. With strategic thinking and the creation of meaningful designs, the studio has built an international reputation for crafting high-quality solutions.

bureaurabensteiner.at

Cameron Haid

Cameron Haid is a graphic designer living and working in Pittsburgh, Pennsylvania.

behance.net/CameronHaid

Ethan Fender

Ethan Fender is an American graphic designer.

dribbble.com/ethnfndr

P144

Evan Wijaya

Evan Wijaya is a graphic designer based in Indonesia. He designs visual identities, illustrations, editorials, packaging and more. He is passionate about projects that involve history, culture and science. His current interest lies in graphic design for films as well as film production and set design.

evanwijaya.com

P070–071, 104–105, 162–163

Farrel Nobel

Farrel Nobel is an Indonesian graphic designer specializing in branding and identity design for small businesses.

behance.net/farrelnobel

P242

Federica Marziale Iadevaia

Federica Marziale Iadevaia is an Italian graphic designer, currently based in Milan, who specializes in editorial design, branding and web design.

behance.net/federicamad19a

P204–205

FourPlus Studio

FourPlus Studio is a creative studio that specializes in motion graphics and identity. They are based in Sofia, Bulgaria and work with clients across the globe. They believe that trust is at the heart of good relationships and this is truly reflected in the quality of their work.

fourplus.bg

P084–085

Gökçe Yiğit

Gökçe Yiğit is an architect and graphic designer based in Istanbul, Turkey.

behance.net/gokceyigit

P132

Graphasel Design Studio

Based in Budapest, Hungary, Graphasel Design Studio is always eager to create more than mere design and strive to find the best possible means of implementation. Their goal is to build well-functioning visual communications projects that have as much creative appeal as purpose.

graphasel.com

P178

Gregor Pogačnik

Gregor Pogačnik is a 20-year-old self-taught digital designer based in Ljubljana, Slovenia.

www2.arnes.si/~gpoga/

P173

Gwen Yixin Zhang

Gwen Yixin Zhang is a human-centered designer based in New York City.

gwenyixinzhang.com

P150–151

Heimlo Studio

Heimlo Studio is a multi-disciplinary design studio based in Jakarta, Indonesia, founded in 2012. Heimlo is known for illustration and graphic design, expressing a distinctively playful, modern Indonesian style through stationery and educational items related to children, art and the city.

heimlo.com

P086–087

Hiroe Nakamura

Hiroe Nakamura entered Musashino Art University in 2003 and began working in a design office in 2007. She started her business as a freelance graphic designer in 2013 in Tokyo, Japan.

behance.net/hireonakamura

P019

Hongjian Li

HongjianLi is an enthusiastic visual designer who loves sports, sneakers and music. He holds a master's degree in graphic design from the Maryland Institute College of Art and a bachelor's degree in visual communication design from Arizona State University.

li-hongjian.com

P176–177

Ilia Savonkin

Ilia Savonkin was born in New York City and raised in Moscow. He is a designer who graduated from the Wordshop Academy of Communications in Russia.

behance.net/ilia_savonkin

P158–159

INVADE

INVADE is a branding studio based in Medellin, Colombia. They strive to create aesthetic, bold and communicative projects using custom types and self-made images.

madebyinvade.com

P226–227, 248

Jacek Walesiak

Jacek Walesiak is a Polish graphic designer and co-founder of the design studio UVMW Warsaw.

uv-warsaw.com

P180–181

Janz Design

Janz Design is a German design studio founded by Nikolai Janz, hence the name. Nikolai is a passionate graphic designer specializing in branding and illustration with a high level of simplicity and diligence. He creates unique graphics by using simple lines and geometric shapes.

janz.design

P182

Jasmina Zornic

Jasmina Zornic is a design director based in Belgrade, Serbia. She is fond of letters, prints, vectors and textures.

behance.net/jasminazornic

P214–215

Jay Cover

Jay Cover is an illustrator born on the Isle of Man, now living and working in Hastings on the South Coast of England. He is one-third of Nous Vous, a collective of artists and illustrators.

jaycover.com

P146–147

JEROME AND ZIMMERMAN

JEROME AND ZIMMERMAN is an award-winning studio and creative firm, producing communication strategies and campaigns, packaging and label design, corporate identities and publishing design, as well as extraordinary print work.

jnz.mx

P196–197

Jérôme Masi

Jérôme Masi is a French art director and illustrator. He has been working as a freelancer for 12 years.

jeromemasi.com

P135

Kata Moravszki

Kata Moravszki is a graphic designer and illustrator based in Budapest, Hungary.

behance.net/katamoravszki

P088–089

illustrations, package design and branding for clients around the world.

smirapdesigns.com

P126–127

Mohammad Rasoulipour

Mohammad Rasoulipour is a designer from Kansas City.

behance.net/Rasoulipour

P142–143

Muhammed Sajid

Muhammed Sajid is a designer based in Bangalore, India.

behance.net/muhammedsajid

P136–137

MUSA WORKLAB

MUSA WORKLAB is a multi-disciplinary design and communication consultancy studio founded in 2003 by Raquel Viana, Paulo Lima and Ricardo Alexandre and located in Lisbon, Portugal. Their focus is to be unconventional, to innovate, to go beyond traditional studio work by integrating an international creative professionals' network with diverse backgrounds and talents.

musaworklab.com

P032

MUTI

MUTI is a creative studio founded in 2011 and based in Cape Town, South Africa. They are a dedicated team of illustrators and designers who are passionate about producing original and inspiring artwork, from lettering to icons, digital painting to animation.

studiomuti.co.za

P133

Nazlıcan Turan

Nazlıcan Turan is a freelance graphic designer who graduated from the department of graphic design at Çukurova University, Turkey.

behance.net/nazlicanturan

P164–165

Nicholai Møller

Nicholai Møller is a designer and vintage lover from Copenhagen, Denmark.

facebook.com/nicholaimoeller/

P243–244

O.OO

The Taipei City, Taiwan, China-based design studio O.OO was formed by two graphic designers. They are dedicated to creating designs that are experimental and use Risograph printing technology.

odotoo.com

P094–095

Old Friend

Old Friend is a branding studio founded by Elliott Snyder and Jesse Morrow. They partner with brands that they believe in and are excited to spur forward, creatively. They get to know the clients, get down to the core of who they are and what they are passionate about, then give movement to it through photography and design.

oldfriend.co

P242

Olga Vasik

Olga Vasik is an award-winning designer and lettering artist from Russia with an eye for detail and a tendency to constantly experiment.

dribbble.com/olgavasik

P080–081

One More

One More is a Shenzhen, China-based design studio founded in 2013. It is a member of the Shenzhen Graphic Design Association.

behance.net/jn94088

P152–153

Paperlux Studio

Paperlux Studio, based in the Schanzenviertel District of Hamburg, Germany, was founded in 2006 by a remarkably unconventional team of branding experts, purebred designers, material fetishists and project wizards.

paperlux.com

P038–039

Paprika

Paprika is a graphic design and strategic marketing firm specializing in business communications services: corporate identity programs, branding, annual reports, brochures, catalogs, posters, packaging, environmental design, signs and websites. Paprika has won more than 800 national and international awards for design excellence since opening its doors for business in 1991.

paprika.com

P120–121, 140–141, 148

Partee

Partee works on the development of graphic and creative solutions to help companies, organizations and individuals communicate their values, products or ideas. They are working to promote a sustainable model that adapts to the new times.

partee.cat

P018

pfp, disseny

pfp, disseny is a Barcelona, Spain-based graphic design studio founded by Quim Pintó and Montse Fabregat in 1990. They work on corporate identity, communication strategy, editorial, exhibition and signage projects.

pfpdisseny.com

P212–213

Plau

Plau is a type and branding studio based in Rio de Janeiro, Brazil. As a full-time type foundry, Plau's typefaces are available from well-known font distributors, such as MyFonts, YouWorkForThem and Fontspring.

plau.co

P192–193

Power-nap Over Design Studio

Power-nap Over Design Studio is a Hong Kong, China-based design studio founded in 2013. Its founder, Vita Mak, completed his bachelor of arts degree in graphic design at the Royal Melbourne Institute of Technology. Vita believes that design is a tool of social change or, at the very least, a means to influence people's thoughts about living.

powernapover.com

P208–209

Quan+Duong

Tri Quan Duong and Ha Duong Nguyen are a creative duo that has a big passion for design and branding. They have built brand identities for many local businesses over the years. They believe that design is a process of creating meaningful works that can make an impact.

behance.net/quanddee

P225

Quatrième Étage

Quatrième Étage is a graphic design studio based in Toulouse, France that specializes in art direction, graphic design and illustration.

quatrieme-etage.com

P090–091

Sylvain Toulouse

Sylvain Toulouse is a Montreal, Canada-based freelance art director and graphic designer. He specializes in visual identity development and logo design, but offers a full spectrum of graphic design services for both the print and digital fields.

sylvaintoulouse.com

P224

Sylvia Baosh

Sylvia Baosh is a Polish-born graphic designer based in Venice, Italy. She mainly focuses on visual identity projects. She studied graphic design at the Università Iuav di Venezia. Currently, she works as an independent graphic designer in partnership with Studio L'ERA and Allison Zurfluh.

behance.net/baosh

P210–211

Tamer Koseli

In 2010, Tamer Koseli founded his studio in Istanbul, Turkey. So far, he has had the privilege of working with companies such as Air Canada, Condé Nast, National Geographic, Men's Health and more.

tamerkoseli.com

P246–247

Taylor Design Works

Taylor Design Works is a design studio in Minnesota. They use design as a tool for solving complex communication problems.

taylordesignworks.com

P057

The Workbench

The Workbench is a graphic design and illustration studio based in Singapore. Since 2014, they have had the pleasure to work on a wide spectrum of projects from the outrageous and fun to the sleek and serious for clients around the world.

theworkbench.sg

P064–069

Thomas Mayfried

Thomas Mayfried is a photographer, graphic designer, publisher and curator. His independent, Munich, Germany-based studio mainly works with cultural and educational institutions and specializes in cooperating with artists.

mayfried.de

P124

Thomas O'Brien

Thomas O'Brien likes graphic design and photography. He is studying communication design at the Royal Melbourne Institute of Technology.

thomobrien.com

P160

Tiago Sá

Tiago Sá is a graphic and web designer based in Lisbon, Portugal.

i-am-tiago.com

P220

Ti-Ming Chu Workshop

Ti-Ming Chu Workshop was founded in 2014. The workshop specializes in combining types and images to explore daily emotions and mainly focuses on visual identity, editorial design, art direction and so on.

behance.net/timingchu

P074

Tricota Agency

Tricota Agency is a multidisciplinary design agency. They design with simplicity, communicate with accuracy and work with custom-made spirit.

tricota.com.ar

P221

Trongtran

Trongtran is a freelance graphic designer who is deeply interested in nature and has a great love for it.

behance.net/TRONGTRANDESIGN88

P078–079

TSUBAKI STUDIO

Tsubaki is the Japanese word for camellia, the flower associated with good luck. With this in mind, TSUBAKI has grown by leaps and bounds in 10 years, imparting knowledge to their clients on branding, communications and marketing along the way.

tsubakistudio.net

P116

Utopia

Utopia is a multifunctional creative brand agency focusing on changing the values of brands, people and the planet.

utopia.agency

P168–169

Why

Why is an independent design consultancy based in London. Since 2003, they have been helping brands meet the challenges they face in their connected world.

wearewhy.agency

P062–063

Wisnu Cipto

Wisnu Cipto is a designer from Bandung, Indonesia.

behance.net/Fatteh

P240–241

Yinsen

Yinsen is a creative studio based in Valencia, Spain and formed by Maria Pradera and Lorena Sayavera.

yinsenstudio.com

P230

Youri V. Kiangala

Youri V. Kiangala is a multidisciplinary graphic designer and photographer based in Eindhoven, The Netherlands.

instagram.com/madebyvieira

P161

Yu-Qian Huang

Yu-Qian Huang is a Taipei City, Taiwan, China-based designer born in 1994.

behance.net/HuangYuQian

P100–101

Zofia Stybor

Zofia Stybor is a graphic designer and fresh graduate from the Academy of Fine Art in Łódź, Poland.

behance.net/zofiastybor

P186

Acknowledgements

We would like to express our gratitude to all of the designers and artists for their generous contributions of images, ideas and concepts. We are also very grateful to many other people whose names do not appear in the credits, but who made specific contributions and provided support. Without them, the successful compilation of this book would not have been possible. Special thanks to all of the contributors for sharing their innovation and creativity with all of our readers around the world.